For Pe

Educating
Grandma

*For Frank and the family
and in memory of those who are gone,
and anticipating those still to come.*

Educating Grandma

by
Winnie Bridges

FALLING WALL PRESS

Educating Grandma published by Falling Wall Press
First published June 1988

Typeset by Camelot Typesetters, Bristol
Printed and bound in Great Britain by Billing & Sons Ltd.,
Worcester
Jacket printed by Doveton Press Ltd., Bristol
Jacket designed by Jean Miller of Studio B, Bristol

The photograph of Mrs Seed is reproduced by kind permission of
the *Lancashire Evening Telegraph*. The author and publishers are
grateful to Geoff Rumney of that newspaper for putting them in
touch with each other.

British Library Cataloguing in Publication Data
Bridges, Winnie
    Educating grandma.
    1. Adult education —England
    1. Title
    374' .942'0924   LC5256.G7

ISBN 0-905046-30-7

Falling Wall Press Ltd.
11 Colston Yard, Colston Street, Bristol BS1 5BD, England

Contents

Illustrations

Acknowledgements

My thanks to Shirley Brown for her help and advice during the writing of this book, and to Dorothy for being so persuasive in 1974.

W.B.
March 1988

CHAPTER ONE

HOW IT ALL BEGAN

When I left school in the summer of 1943 at the age of thirteen years and forty-nine weeks, I believed that going to work at the local leatherworks must be just about the most exciting thing that was ever likely to happen to me. I would start putting my hair up in metal curling-pins every night like a proper working girl, and make my stubbornly straight, thick red hair into what I imagined was a glamorous, shining pageboy like Ginger Rogers's. And I would be able to go to the pictures two or three times a week, funds and not parents permitting. I pitied my fellow school-leavers who were 'goin' into t'mill' to learn to weave, wind or cotton — the traditional means of earning a living for Lancashire cashire's womenfolk — and I had no envy for those who had found themselves 'posh' jobs in offices or shops. They belonged for the most part to what my mother called 't'better end', and I had never aspired to that, although the headmistress of Our Lady and St. Hubert's Roman Catholic Elementary School, which I had attended from the age of three, had suggested rather wistfully that, being good at English, I might be able to find work in an office. As far as I was concerned, office work was for those whose parents sat in the front pews in church every Sunday, and t'mill was fit only for those whose parents worked on the premise that 'wot's allus bin good enough for me's good enough for thee an' that's all there is to it.'

The leatherworks was not quite the Utopia I had hoped for. The hours were long and the work was tiring for a skinny, not very strong fourteen-year-old. Instead of staying up till all hours, I was often only too glad to be in my bed by nine o'clock. The older girls at work smiled, I knew, at my naive attempts to emulate their sophisticated ways with the boys who worked alongside us in the 'big room'; while the boys, far from seeing in me Great Harwood's answer to Hollywood's Ginger Rogers, obviously regarded my

7

childish looks as beneath their notice, except to point out that the
school was up the road and 't'leatherworks were no place for
little lasses'. I quickly discovered that adult life had few charms for
a factory girl like myself, and the best bit about it was pay-day.
Every Friday night, I proudly took home to my mother my unopen-
ed wage packet containing £1.6s.8d (£1.33) and was given a whole
half-crown (12½p) spending money for myself, which made me
feel that I was really grown-up. It cost only ninepence (4p+) to
go into either of the town's two cinemas, and only sixpence (2½p)
− a child's admission price − for someone who looked as young
as I did, so a half-crown could be stretched quite a long way.
I *was* rather crestfallen the first time I asked for a ninepenny
ticket and the woman in the box office laughed,
obviously thinking I was *pretending* to be grown-up; but, since
she laughed every time I asked for a ninepenny ticket, I gave in
and bought sixpenny tickets until long after my fifteenth birthday.

In those days, fourteen was considered quite old enough for
working-class children to be earning a living. After all, most of
our parents, including my own, had been 'half-timers'* in the mills
at the age of twelve and full-timers at thirteen. Further education
was virtually unheard of in our world and secondary education
was only for those whose parents could afford to pay for it, or for
those who passed the scholarship examinations at the age of eleven.
At St. Hubert's Girls', only three pupils were chosen each year
to sit the scholarship and, as I was not one of them during my
year in Standard Four, I knew that, at fourteen, I would leave
school and go to work along with the great majority of my
schoolmates. The general feeling among working people at that
time was that the ability to reckon up their wages, write an
adequate letter and read a popular newspaper or magazine was all
the education necessary to equip their children for working life.
That is not to say that most working people had no interests

---

* The half-time system evolved from the 1844 Factory Act, which restricted
  children to working officially a maximum of six and a half hours a day, with
  three hours in school. By the beginning of the present century, such children
  spent half of each day in school and half working in the mill, hence the term
  'half-timers'. The system finally ended in 1921.

outside the factory, workshop or coal-mine. Our local library was very well used; music societies, glee clubs and rambling associations thrived, along with many other social organisations run by local schools, churches and groups of individuals with a common interest. But, in small towns like Great Harwood, where cotton had been the staple industry for generations, working-class children went into the mill or factory, and we tended to think of reading as something to do in our spare time. Both my parents were avid readers and my mother encouraged us children with the words: 'You'll never be lonely while you can read a good book; you can pass many a happy hour reading if you ever find yourself alone.'

When I began at the leatherworks, the Second World War was in its fourth year. My father worked as a coal-miner at that time and my mother, unlike the mothers of many of my friends, did not work outside the home, which was a comfortable terraced house in a street of similar houses. I was the third of four children, two boys and two girls. Dick, the elder of my two brothers, was then eighteen and serving in the Royal Navy. Our younger brother, Arnold, had drowned in an accident in the winter of 1942 when he was only fourteen, and so only my twelve-year-old sister Betty and I were at home with our parents. In our little town, the War sometimes seemed more like a series of celebrations than the time of mass slaughter it was. To us children, it meant exciting days when our brother, uncles or cousins came home on leave, bringing with them extra supplies of sweets and chocolate; the coming of the evacuees from Manchester with their big city cockiness and a lack of respect for their elders and betters that left us bewildered; and fund-raising events like War Weapons Week and Wings for Victory Week, with concerts and parties arranged by local organisations and, most exciting of all, military parades through our main streets with brass bands and flag-waving crowds and the exotic-looking Commonwealth troops from the barracks in the larger towns nearby. After listening to the news on the BBC's Home Service on her relay wireless set, with the triumphant voice of the newsreader giving details of many enemy casualties, my mother's cheerful face would grow serious and she would say quietly, 'They're all somebody's lads.'

Then, when it was all over and the real celebrations had ended, we settled back into the small-town world we had always known and − except for those who mourned their lost loved ones, and those who had seen things they wanted to try to forget − it was almost as if nothing had happened.

During the years between my leaving school at fourteen and marriage at twenty, my parents began to think me a bit of a flibberty-gibbet. In our town in the 1940s, people prided themselves − and some still do − on the number of years they had worked for one firm. But within six years, I had moved from the leatherworks to the Oxo factory, from there to the slipperworks, then on to a small jersey mill, where I was taught to wind yarn from cones on to bobbins. I never disgraced myself by getting the sack, but my rebellious streak meant that sometimes I escaped it only by the skin of my teeth. Unlike many of my workmates, I simply could not keep my mouth shut when something unfair happened, whether to me or to someone I worked with. At the slipperworks I had soon found myself on the wrong side of the manager. Then one day we were shifted to another department where we had to do a job that involved standing at benches. One elderly lady had difficulty standing, so I found her a box to sit on just the right height so she could sit down and work. The foreman did not like that, and was going to make her stand up, so we all went down to see the manager. I spoke out of turn, and he got as far as saying 'And as for you . . .' before I got in first with 'I'm going for me cards.'

By the time of my marriage in 1950, I had become a four-loom weaver at Palatine Mill, having learned to weave at the age of nineteen in their new weaving school. Assured by older, experienced operatives that I now had a 'trade in my fingers' that would guarantee me a job for life, I quite enjoyed the feeling of autonomy that came from the possession of 'my own' four looms, and the knowledge that the piece-work system of payment meant that I was responsible to some degree for the size of my pay packet. The Palatine was known as a 'comfortable' place to work − the workers there were friendly and the management left us to get

on with it without too much officious supervision, unlike some
of the places I had worked in – and experience had taught me
that my patronising pity for my contemporaries who had gone
straight from school to t'mill had been wasted. Monotonous work
was monotonous work no matter where you did it, and the
important thing was how much you were paid for it. Weaving
compared favourably, in this respect, with the other jobs I had
done: my four looms earned me around five pounds a week, a
respectable amount for a woman at that time. The camaraderie
in the mill, and the helpfulness of my 'partners' – those who
worked next to me in the weaving shed – lightened the monotony,
and I was content enough.

I met Frank when I was eighteen and I really fell for him. I
had gone with friends to the local roller-skating rink where my
disastrous efforts to skate had landed me in a heap at his feet. He
helped me up and we were soon meeting regularly. He would come
over on the bus from Clitheroe, his home town some seven miles
away, every Saturday and Sunday night and on alternate
Wednesdays, for he worked shifts in a Clitheroe mill. The
Wednesday evening meetings were a sure sign in our society that
his intentions were serious since, for some reason, Wednesday
was regarded as the official 'courting night'. Before many weeks
had passed, I took him to meet the family and his feet were firmly
planted 'under t'table' as we say in these parts. He was my first
and only steady boyfriend, and we courted for over two years until
my mother solved our problem of how to tell her I was pregnant
by confronting us with the fact that she already knew. Dressed
in blue 'jigger coat', silky print dress, white court shoes and pale
blue beanie hat, I was married on a hot June morning to my
handsome young lover, who now worked as a farm labourer and
had been given a single day off for the occasion. Most weddings
were on a Saturday, but I could not even get married on the right
day. An administrative muddle between the Register Offices of
Blackburn and Clitheroe meant we had to get a special licence
and marry on a Monday instead of the previous Saturday as
planned. At half-past eight I was washing lettuce for the breakfast,
at nine o'clock I was making my vows in St. Hubert's Church,

and after the feast Frank and I went off to Blackpool for the day.
On the Tuesday, he was back at the farm and I was back at my
looms.

In September 1950, to our great delight, our son Frank was born.
We had made our first home with my parents, who both welcomed
this first grandson — my brother Dick and his wife, Susan, already
had two small daughters — with such obvious pleasure that the
inauspicious start to our marriage no longer mattered. Within three
years I also had a daughter, Mary, and a second son, David, which
meant we qualified for one of the new council houses on the
outskirts of the town. Work was still plentiful in our area and,
as our family increased, Frank took various jobs with plenty of
overtime, and I took whatever part-time work came up as and when
I could, to help supplement the budget and keep our children
clothed and fed. My mother, plump, cheerful and capable, was
always willing to help care for the children and they were never
left alone or with strangers. She became our best friend and the
children adored her.

In April 1963, on my mother's seventieth birthday, our eleventh
and last child, Maureen, was born. We now had four sons and
seven daughters under the age of thirteen. As a girl I had often
entertained a rosy dream of being the mother of a large and loving
family. Large and loving the family certainly were, but the reality
of being their mother was often a great deal less than rosy.
Fortunately, I was blessed with good health and a sense of humour,
two qualities which stood me in good stead throughout those years
when the children were young. Now, whenever I am asked how
on earth I coped with my large family and the washing, cooking,
cleaning, ironing, shopping and all the other chores of family life,
I find it very difficult to describe exactly what life was like during
those hectic years. The children, and the work of caring for them,
were facts of life and there was no time to stop and analyse my
methods of coping with them all. I have never been particularly
houseproud, which, in the circumstances, was just as well, since
it would have been impossible to keep our four-bedroomed council
house permanently spick and span. So long as the place was
reasonably clean and tidy and the children were happy and

well-fed, I never worried overmuch about a little dust here and there or a few toys cluttering up the place.

As the children grew older, both girls and boys were expected to earn their spending money by helping in the house. They kept their bedrooms tidy; took turns with the washing up in the evenings and with cleaning the bathroom and kitchen; helped to prepare the vegetables; shopped for small things; and even the youngest ones would tidy the shoe cupboard and dry the spoons. Frank did the gardening and decorating and I did the washing, ironing and cooking. In short, we all 'mucked in' and none of us was any the worse for our efforts. We had a large garden at the back, with a narrow one running the length of the house. Behind the old people's bungalows opposite was a fairly large plot of land which Frank rented from the Council and used to grow enough vegetables to last us for eight or nine months of the year. He loved gardening and, no matter how long his hours at work, always found time to tend his plants so expertly that for several years as an active member of the local horticultural society he won many prizes at their annual shows, for both flowers and vegetables.

Christmas was always a wonderful time, with each child receiving one 'big' present — a doll and pram or a tricycle or pedal car — for which we would be making weekly payments for months before and, occasionally, even afterwards, together with several smaller ones: books, games and the like. Every year, Frank would bring home the 'pick box'. He would spend four or five pounds to fill a large cardboard box with sweets and chocolate bars — Rolos, fruit pastilles, packets of jelly babies, licorice all-sorts, dolly mixtures, Maltesers, Mars bars and so on. Each child was supposed to have one 'pick' a day from the box during the two-week Christmas holiday, and beyond if the sweets lasted long enough. But every year without fail, temptation would prove too strong and, whilst I was busy upstairs or in the kitchen, young Frank, always the leader, would organise a raid on the box and all the favourite sweets would disappear. Frank would vow that next year there would be no 'pick box' — but there always was.

We usually managed to have a large turkey and at least three chickens for dinner. I would spend Christmas Eve cooking these, and baking dozens of jam tarts and mince pies, preparing jellies and trifles and peeling pounds of potatoes so that I could spend as much time as possible on Christmas Day in the living-room with the rest of the family. All the children went to bed early and without complaint on Christmas Eve so that Father Christmas would bring them the presents they hoped for. Even after they stopped believing in him, the older ones enacted this ritual for the sake of the little ones, and I believe they continued to enjoy it for its own sake as a family tradition. Frank loved it all, from trimming the tree and festooning the walls with gaily coloured paper garlands to setting out the presents in a separate pile for each child. Around midnight the two of us would find ourselves standing in the middle of the room, surrounded by toys, wishing each other a 'Happy Christmas', and complaining in mock dismay that we had nowhere to sit, for every seat was piled high with presents.

On Christmas morning, Frank would be up long before seven to light the fires in the living-room and kitchen. He would then bring me up a cup of tea, by which time the children were clamouring to come downstairs. Young Frank, by virtue of his position as eldest, would line up all his brothers and sisters, youngest first, at the head of the stairs. Then, arms spread wide to keep any one of them from coming down out of turn, he would wait for my signal before dropping his arms to let them come down one by one, with himself bringing up the rear. Once they were downstairs, pandemonium reigned as bicycle bells rang, car horns blew and baby dolls called plaintively for 'Mamma'. My parents always came to us for Christmas Day, and my mother would tell them 'You're t'luckiest chilther in 'Arrod', doubtless remembering her own childhood and the Christmas dolls hanging upon the wall that she and her sisters were never allowed to play with. These were magical times and well worth the post-Christmas empty purse.

We were happy but it was a struggle to keep the family ship on an even keel. As every parent will know, the older children grow, the more they need and demand. Inexplicably, all their shoes seemed to wear out at the same time; some evenings I would be washing socks and vests and trying to dry them in time for school the following morning. On one never-to-be-forgotten day, Eileen

and Margaret, then aged seven and a half and six, wailed that their
knicker elastic had mysteriously vanished during the night. Anne
and Kathleen, aged ten and nine, had become enamoured of a new
form of skipping, known as 'Chinese skipping', for which lengths
of elastic were required, and had purloined the necessary from
the underwear of their young sisters. While the boys laughed
gleefully and the victims and culprits — the last two suitably
chastised — wept into their cornflakes, I dashed upstairs to search
for the missing elastic, which I found tucked under the mattress
of the guilty pair. Knotted, twisted and filthy, it was useless for
its true purpose. Even worse, its length revealed that it had once
held up several pairs of knickers. Poor little Eileen and Margaret
owned not one pair of elasticated knickers between them and were
forced to become 'pin-up girls' for the day until the elastic could
be replaced.

Not all our disasters were so comic. Coping with multiple cases
of measles, chicken-pox and other such childhood illnesses was
no laughing matter. Then there were the accidents that are bound
to occur in a family as large as ours, like the day eleven-year-old
Mary went out for five minutes and didn't come back for a week
— proving she could do whatever her brothers could do, she had
climbed further than them on to a mill roof, fallen through it and
landed herself in hospital; and the day eight-year-old Kevin threw
a stone over a bridge and forgot to let go. Both suffered only minor
injuries, and we thought ourselves lucky.

As the years passed and the children became more independent
of me, I began to take more interest in the world outside the home.
I found time to read the newspapers, to listen to the radio news
and discussion programmes which had been just another
background noise of family life, and to form opinions which, being
me, I could not keep to myself. I started writing letters to the local
evening paper on such diverse topics as luminous road safety
armbands for schoolchildren, the meagreness of the old age
pension, anomalies in the Social Security system, and anything
that set me off. The letters were often published and always
produced strong reactions, both for and against. Acquaintances

would stop me in the street to compliment me on my letter-writing skills and, occasionally, to thank me for expressing beliefs and opinions they shared. I also began to write a little poetry again, something I had enjoyed doing as a child, but which I had almost forgotten about since leaving school. Initially, my new attempts at verse consisted of a few humorous lines to amuse my workmates, or anniversary and birthday card verses written on request. As time went on, I began to write more seriously, the poems reflecting my thoughts on the children, topical questions and life in general. During the quiet hours when the family were in bed, I carefully copied my efforts into an exercise book, which was soon filled. A spate of assaults on young children prompted me to write a poem for my own children, and those of friends, on the dangers of speaking to strangers. A friend sent it to a local weekly paper, the *Blackburn Times,* and this resulted in publication of the poem and a visit from a reporter from that newspaper and one from the *Lancashire Evening Telegraph.* A local printer, an acquaintance of Frank's, suggested that he might print a selection of my poems in booklet form to be sold at a nominal price, 'just to see if they'll sell'. *A Random Collection of Poems* at 1s.6d (7½p) sold several hundred copies, and was followed by *Poems: A Second Volume* at 2s (10p), which was equally popular.*

By the early 1970s my writing had gained me something of a reputation and I was no longer just ''er on th'estate wi' all them children'. Because of all this, my friend Dorothy thought me a likely candidate to fill a place on the English Literature O level course that she and some of her friends wanted to take at evening classes.

'If it's under-subscribed,' she pleaded, 'they won't run it and I know you'd enjoy it.'

'But I'm on shift work and I'll only be able to go alternate weeks,' I protested. 'Besides, I'll never be able to do an O level. Our Frank used to spend hours in the dining-room swotting for his O levels. He used to bring home piles of homework, too. I know I'd only be doing one, but I work full-time as well as

* See Appendix C for some examples.

everything else I have to do; I've hardly time to spit out as it is!'

But Dorothy persisted.

'Look, I'll make sure you get the notes on the nights you can't make it. You know how you like reading and you're good at English to start with. You could walk an O level if you put your mind to it; you'll probably show the rest of us up!'

With such devious flattery Dorothy got her way and I agreed to enrol for the classes the following Monday. And that is how, in the dusk of a September evening in 1974, Frank came to be escorting a somewhat dubious student-to-be up the hill to the local Council School which housed the Adult Centre where the enrolment session was held. As we neared the building, I had the curious feeling that my schooldays were catching up with me, for every Monday afternoon from the age of eleven, together with the rest of my classmates, I had left the familiar classrooms of St. Hubert's Girls' to attend this very school for lessons in laundry, cookery and something 'they' called housewifery, which seemed to consist of little except cleaning greasy gas ovens and giving the headmaster's study a 'thorough turnout'. I always felt quite indignant about this particular task, partly because of an ingrained dislike of having to use 'elbow grease' for any purpose whatsoever, and partly because I saw no reason why St. Hubert's Catholic Girls' School should provide skivvies for the headmaster of a non-Catholic mixed school. Memories of those days flickered vaguely through my mind as we went through the iron gates and crossed the concrete playground towards the side door. This led to the steep flights of stone steps which had once guided my reluctant feet to the laundry room where we girls had spent whole afternoons washing perhaps a tea towel and a couple of hankies: soaking, scrubbing, rinsing, drying, ironing in strict rotation as if our very lives depended on the cleanliness of the ragged items we had persuaded our mothers to trust us with. The laundry teacher, a small, thin woman of indeterminate age, had a voice like a whip.

'Girls. Why do we soak our handkerchiefs in cold water with plenty of salt?'

'To remove the mucus, Miss Sagar.'

I longed to say 'Because they're snotty like you, Miss', but her hand was as stinging as her tongue, as I had discovered when she caught me drinking the mouthful of milk that remained from my scone mixture (she also taught cookery) and she had slapped my face. The fact that the milk was included in the twopence I had paid for my ingredients stung me more than the slap.

Now, over thirty years later, I re-entered this room to find that the deep sinks which had lined two sides of it, and over which we girls had laboured, were no longer there; nor were the wooden rubbing-boards and the huge stoves where we had heated the flat-irons used to smooth our laundry on the long, scrubbed table that had stood on stout legs in the centre of the room. In their place were several small tables. Behind each of these stood a blackboard, upon which a course title was chalked. In front of each blackboard and behind each table sat the course tutors, some busily enrolling potential students, others waiting hopefully for someone to show interest in their courses. Frank, not wishing to be taken for a prospective student, hovered by the door while I went in search of the English Literature tutor. I had not realised how much my eyesight had deteriorated over the years, helped, no doubt, by the fluorescent lights which were on all day in the windowless winding-room of the mill where I now worked. The information on the boards was just a blur of chalk to me and, too vain to admit that I could not see properly, I wandered about the room, peering at the boards in the hope that I might recognise the magic words 'English Literature'. Fortunately, my attempts failed to fool a former schoolmate of mine: 'If you're looking for Sociology,' she said, 'you're in the right queue.'

'Sociology? You must be joking!' I exclaimed, retreating hurriedly to the opposite side of the room. Sociology was just a word to me, and a mysterious one at that. Thankful for my escape, I gave up on vanity and walked towards a large, balding young man who was standing by one of the blackboards.

'Could you please tell me where I can enrol for English Literature?'

He looked at the blackboard and then at me in disbelief. How could anyone who was obviously half-blind, or unable to read, possibly hope to study English Literature? his eyes seemed to ask.

But he politely told me that he was the English Literature tutor, gave me an enrolment form and discreetly left me to complete it. Having done this, I handed back the form, paid him in advance for the first ten weeks' tuition and, trying my best to look dignified, made my way to the door where Frank stood waiting for me. Gratefully, I took his arm and allowed him to guide me down the steps and out of the building where my formal education was soon to begin again.*

* See Appendix B.

CHAPTER TWO

CHANGING TIMES, A MARCH – AND JUNE

Two weeks after enrolling for the English Literature course, I found myself once more climbing the steps to the former laundry room for the first class. This time I was alone, but I was relieved to find that Dorothy had already arrived and had kept a place for me beside her in the second row. She introduced me to the group of friends she had mentioned when she had asked me to join the class, and we settled down to pay attention as Peter, the course tutor, stood beside the blackboard and began to speak. Since realising the poor state of my eyesight, I had been rather anxious at the thought of having to read from the blackboard. Foolishly, I had stilled my fears by telling myself that it was unlikely that adult education teachers would use the blackboard all that much, for surely we would not be expected to copy work from the board in the way we children had done at St. Hubert's. I was to find later that I had been right: Peter's lessons were mainly discussion with a little dictation. However, during those first moments as he began to read the list of books on the syllabus, simultaneously writing them on the board for us to copy, my heart sank and I wondered how I would cope if this was his usual teaching method.

Somehow I managed to scribble the titles in the small pocket notebook I had brought with me: *The Lost World of the Kalahari* by Laurens van der Post; Shakespeare's *Romeo and Juliet;* Conrad's *The Rover;* an anthology of poems; Harold Owen's *Journey from Obscurity; Wuthering Heights* by Emily Brontë; and Thomas Hardy's *Far From the Madding Crowd.* Where, I asked myself, was I going to get all these books from? And, more to the point, when would I find time to read them? Memories of happy hours spent with Catherine Cookson, Agatha Christie and Jean Plaidy when the children were in bed or following their own interests were replaced by the prospect of ploughing my way with difficulty through what seemed to me a formidable list of works with which to begin my new hobby. Then I remembered Dorothy's words: 'We can have a laugh and we don't need to sit the exam if we don't feel up to it.' She was right. I was here to enjoy myself, not to be tested on my reading ability with a stern teacher waiting to pounce on my every mistake. Anyway, there was nothing wrong with my reading ability – I cannot recall a time when I was unable to read. These books were different, of course, from the popular fiction I was used to; but, given time, I would get used to them, too. I might even begin to enjoy them . . .

My attention returned to Peter as he launched into a synopsis of Shakespeare's life and times. When he stopped to sketch a rough model of the Globe Theatre on the board I panicked again, but this time only briefly, for Christine, the girl on my left, was drawing the model on an A4-size pad, and I managed to make a copy of sorts, albeit a bit lop-sided. Peter's enthusiasm for Shakespeare was infectious, and I became so absorbed that it was nine o'clock and the end of the first lesson in what seemed no time at all.

The following Monday found me on the late shift watching the bobbins of yarn endlessly spinning round. During the previous week, I had copied out Peter's notes carefully, and had begun to read *The Lost World of the Kalahari* which Mary had borrowed for me from a friend. It was not the kind of book I would have taken from the library shelves, and I was surprised to find that I had no difficulty in understanding what the author was saying and that I really enjoyed reading it. If the other set books were as absorbing as this one, I felt, I would enjoy the course after all. Peter's talk on Shakespeare had certainly been stimulating and now, as I walked round the winding-frame changing a bobbin here and piecing up a broken end there, I felt envious of Dorothy, Christine and the others who were enjoying a second helping of his knowledge whilst I ruined my eyesight staring at those spinning bobbins. I was surprised by my own thoughts and by the stab of envy they had stirred in me. Most of all, I was surprised to realise how eagerly I was looking forward to next Monday when I was on early shift and could attend the class.

My eagerness turned to dismay when the class began and Peter

informed us that we were to begin *Romeo and Juliet,* with each
of us reading a part. As I was still without my own copy of the
text, I had to share with someone. My partner smiled brightly and
said, 'It's a lovely play, isn't it? Not one of the Bard's best, perhaps,
but lovely all the same.' If she hoped for some response she was
disappointed, for I just gazed in panic at the open book and the
words which, to me, were not merely archaic; they were almost
unintelligible. I groaned inwardly. Then Peter began to read and,
as we all read our parts in turn, stilted and mechanical though we
sounded, I began to make sense of the story and to gain some small
degree of confidence, so that by the end of the evening, though
still unsure of the meaning of many of the Shakespearean terms,
I was holding my own and enjoying the experience.

This time, before we left, Peter set us a piece of homework.
We were to write an essay on the reasons behind the tragedy, with
particular reference to Romeo's part in it. When I arrived home,
young Frank was just leaving for his own house five minutes' walk
away.

'How's it going, Mum?' he asked.

'We-ell, better than I expected the first time,' I told him, 'but
can you tell me if an essay's the same thing as a composition?'

He raised his eyes heavenwards. 'Aye, Mum, an essay's just
the same thing as a composition.' Then he smiled warmly. 'And
if anybody can write a good 'un, you can.' And away he went.

The older children had been unanimous in their encouragement
when I had told them about the evening class, Mary even going
so far as to enrol herself at the second session. The younger ones
were less interested at that time, being far more absorbed in the
local disco, the youth club, fashion clothes and pop records. I had
the impression that they thought me slightly mad even to
contemplate doing, of my own free will, something that they were
more or less obliged to do by a system which had begun to demand
paper qualifications for virtually any job they might hope to obtain
on leaving school.

Although my own youthful ambitions as a working-class child
of the 1930s had been almost non-existent, Frank had often spoken
of his early desire to be a professional gardener, a wish thwarted

by his parents' need for him to earn more than was paid to an
apprentice in those days; and so he had remained untrained, taking
a succession of jobs which demanded maximum physical strength
and which paid well. These included foundry work, chimney-
sweeping, fire-stoking at a coke works, mill work and several
others, all of them arduous. Quick to learn new skills and never
afraid of hard work, he had never had much difficulty in finding
a job where the pay, supplemented by my irregular earnings, was
enough to keep our large family well-fed and adequately clothed.
Nevertheless, although our own garden gave him the opportunity
to spend his leisure time doing what he loved best, he remembered
his disappointment and we agreed that our children, when the time
came, would be allowed to choose the means by which they would
earn a living. In our narrow world of small industrial towns, which
had for generations depended on cotton for economic prosperity,
financial security was the main thing we looked for in a job. Our
parents had known the deprivations of the inter-war years, when
the fall in the cotton trade had meant unemployment figures of
over sixty per cent in some of these small towns, including Great
Harwood, and the only recourse for many working people had
been the hated Means Test. So it is not surprising that we valued
a steady, regularly paid job so highly. The conditions in the
factories where Frank and I worked in 1974 did not include
payment for time off sick, nor any of the benefits which even the
lowest-paid professions have long taken for granted. Like most
of our neighbours and acquaintances, we lived from pay-day to
pay-day, saving from our weekly wages the money for household
bills and, if we could afford it, holidays. To many of us, illness
belonged in the same category as holidays – it was a luxury, for,
like our parents before us, the majority of us preferred to 'work
off' our ailments rather than claim State benefits. It was, then,
very important to us that our children should have the choice of
jobs we had never had and if, having made their choice, they were
happy and secure in their work, that was an added bonus.

Very few people in our part of the world considered further
education, unless for vocational training, and our children were
no exception. Young Frank took O levels to qualify for entrance

to the engineering branch of the Royal Navy, which he joined at seventeen soon after leaving school. He had left the Navy after nearly six years, having married Barbara whom he met while stationed in Scotland. He now worked as a plant attendant at a local power station, where pay and conditions were good and where there were prospects for promotion. With this in mind, under a scheme sponsored by his employers, he was studying by correspondence course for the relevant qualifications.

Mary had opted to leave school at fifteen to join the nursing cadet scheme run by a hospital for the mentally subnormal. After a year working on the wards, the cadets began training for their nursing certificates, spending one day in college each week. Mary had left the hospital before qualifying, to take a job in a factory where she could earn more money. At nineteen she left home and went to London, where she worked in a hotel for six months before returning home pregnant with Laura. To say that Frank and I were shocked and upset by her news would be putting it mildly. But we survived the shock, and were delighted when Laura was born. At the time I began attending evening classes, Mary was engaged to John, and she and Laura were living with him and his parents in Great Harwood.

When David left school, he chose a gardening apprenticeship at the same hospital where Mary had started her working life. Anne started a secretarial course at a local college, leaving at seventeen to marry Geoff and have their baby, Andrea. Kathleen did not want a 'dressed up job' and joined a local clothing firm as a trainee sewing machinist. Michael had left his job as an apprentice printer before he was eighteen, to marry and live in Waterfoot with his wife, Jean. Eileen, as Kathleen had done, chose factory work and instant wages in preference to studying for future rewards. Apart from its size, our family was, I suppose, fairly typical of the families in our area. Now, even the four children still at school were becoming more and more independent of me, and the Monday evening classes began to fill a need I had not known I had.

To write my essay on *Romeo and Juliet*, I needed a copy of the play, so I sent an SOS to Mr Sykes, Head of English at the children's school. That evening he sent back not only an excellent edition of the Shakespeare but also a copy of *Wuthering Heights* (which I returned reluctantly at the end of the year). The following Monday, as I walked round the winding-frame piecing up the broken ends and changing the pirns* when they emptied, I could think of little else but the class I was missing. When we ran out of pirns, instead of brushing down the dusty frame and sweeping the floor surrounding it, as the other winders did while waiting for fresh supplies, I took my copy of *Romeo and Juliet* from my bag and sat on a weft box to read it. When next I attended the class and my essay was singled out for praise by Peter, I felt as thrilled as I had been nearly forty years earlier when, at the age of six, I had been given a hollow chocolate Easter egg for completing a year's full attendance at school. No matter that the egg had broken into smithereens when I dropped it rushing home to tell my mother. I had won it and that was what mattered. Peter's praise was the same, only better, for I had enjoyed myself earning it. Dorothy's idea had been a good one after all.

The evening classes soon became the highlights of my life, as much for the people I met as for what I was learning. I found that I actually enjoyed doing the exercises and writing the essays set by Peter, and my good marks gave me the confidence to take an active part in the literary discussions we had in class. Most of my fellow-students had been to grammar schools or secondary moderns, and all seemed to have that confidence in themselves and their opinions that I had previously lacked. Writing to the local paper was quite different from stating my views in front of other people who might disagree and were not afraid to tell me so. I had been brought up to 'know my place', and one of the tenets of knowing your place was not to argue with your 'betters'. All my life, teachers had held a firm place in the army of 'betters' that commanded respect. I remember meeting one of my former teachers as I pushed the pram along the street with two toddlers trailing along behind. I had inclined my head respectfully and

* Pirns are long narrow tubes which fit into the shuttles used to carry the weft across the loom. (Weft is the thread that is fed into the shuttle which crosses the width of the loom when weaving cloth.)

murmured, 'Good morning, Miss Moran,' for all the world as
if I were risking a rap on the knuckles if I didn't!

But here I found I had no betters, or at least none who regarded
themselves so. Peter most certainly did not, nor did any of my
new friends, several of whom came from that very 'better end'
I had so scorned in my youth. They were kind and considerate
people who had the same sort of problems that I had, who worried
just like everybody else, and who enjoyed a good laugh just as
much as the folk in the mill did. I had a feeling that, although
the majority of the mill folk had been very encouraging when they
learned of my new enterprise, one or two of them thought I was
getting a bit above myself. Of course, that could have been my
imagination, but the feeling was undeniably there. I was learning
quite a lot about myself as well as about other people and was
realising that my life, which had seemed so full, was really quite
a narrow one, though undeniably hectic.

After twenty-four years of married life, Frank and I had become
as comfortable together as a pair of old slippers. Although we were
already very happy, our relationship perceptibly changed for the
better through my enthusiasm for the classes. He joined me in
seeking out the books I needed for the course, and we spent several
Saturday afternoons browsing in Seed and Gabbutt's bookshop in
Blackburn, where I discovered Frank's intense interest in the First
World War and its causes. He had often spoken of his Grandad
who had been a veteran of the Battle of the Somme, but I had had
no idea of the extent of his interest until I saw the eagerness with
which he scanned the bookshelves for anything to do with the
1914-1918 War. During those outings, each of us became aware
of the other as a person again, and not just the spouse with whom
we spent the greater part of our lives. I was to learn later that not
all women − or men, for that matter − are as fortunate in the
support of their partners when returning to education, but, for us,
this was a time of renewal in our marriage and we made the most
of it.

My relationship with the children also benefited. Now I felt an
empathy with them in their learning problems and they, in turn,
seemed to find it easier to discuss personal problems with me as

well. At first, they had been amused at my decision to take an O level course, so it was gratifying to find that they were now quite proud of having a Mum who was prepared to have a go at something new. Even my mother, then in her eighties, was interested in how I was faring at 't'neet schoo''.

'Ev they fon' 'im yet?' she would ask, with a twinkle in her eye. 'Romeo, I mean; wherefore were 'e when tha fon' 'im?'

As for myself, my confidence continued to grow. By the time the end of the first term drew near, I was well into my stride and, with Dorothy's help in supplying the notes I missed when on the late shift, I had managed to keep up with the rest of the class and to do all the homework that Peter had set. This included a second essay on the Shakespeare, one on *Far From the Madding Crowd,* and another on T. S. Eliot's 'The Triumphal March' from the poetry anthology. I was surprised and pleased to find that I could not only read, and write about, great writers, but enjoy them. Family and work were no longer the be-all and end-all.

But life at the mill went on much as usual. It was convenient for me to work shifts, in spite of not being able to attend my classes each week. When I was on the two-till-ten shift, I could see the family off to work and school and get my own chores done before going to work. I would do my main cleaning and a big wash during my 'late' weeks, so that the weeks I was on six-till-two were free of all but the everyday tasks. As Frank worked regular night shifts, he slept through the day and the children had dinner at school, so our main meal was eaten in the evening. I would make huge casseroles, stews and hot-pots which could be left to cook slowly in the oven while I was at work. Frank liked to cook occasionally, but was extravagant with ingredients – and with money when shopping for them – so I preferred to do it myself. We all 'mucked in' and shared the housework and, apart from the usual family squabbles over whose turn it was to wash or dry the dishes, or who was last to use the bathroom and, therefore, the one to clean it, we managed quite well. Most of my studying was done late at night when the children were in bed, and at weekends when Frank was gardening and the children busy with their own interests. And instead of letters to the papers or poems for myself, I wrote essays for the classes.

In the winding-room, the work was repetitive and tiring, though
not difficult. I needed the money I earned and Highams Ltd. was
as good a place as any in which to earn it: only two minutes' walk
from home; clean and modern compared with most other places
I had worked in; quite good pay and no-one standing behind me
to see that I earned it. Yet, sometimes I felt as if I were merely
an appendage of the machine, and I am fairly certain that that was
the management's view of me and my fellow-winders. In spite
of these feelings, I cannot deny that the mechanical work had its
compensations, for it made few demands on my mind and I passed
the time thinking my own thoughts and dreaming my own dreams
as I performed the menial tasks required of me. There is a certain
peace and privacy to be found in the noisy heart of a mill, where
the very noise protects you from distractions: lesser sounds go
unnoticed and the passing footsteps of other workers go unheard,
so that you can lose yourself in your own silent world far away
from the din of the factory.

When we ran out of pirns or when the machines broke down,
which happened regularly, there was plenty of entertainment. Our
foreman, or 'winding-master' as he liked to call himself, had a
penchant for bashing the machines with his hammer if something
happened to upset him. A mild-looking man in his late thirties,
his wrath was awesome as he strode down the room to repair a
frame that had dared to break down simply in order to provoke him.

'The bluddy black pig!' he would yell, hammering with
exaggerated anger at the offending machine. 'Bluddy women!
Shouldn't be let loose on t'bluddy machines!'

Occasionally, just for a laugh, I would go into the wooden hut
he called his 'office' and surreptitiously remove the hammer, hide
it and wait for Lily, one of the other winders, to call on his services.
Lily was tall, thin and persistent, caring nothing for the foreman's
temper. In a booming voice that could be heard above the rattle
of the machinery, she would yell, 'De-ennis! It's brokken − Ah
can't do nowt till yer fix it.'

'Wait a minute − I can't find me bluddy 'ammer, can I?' He
would come stomping up the room, dirty white coat flying behind

him, hair awry, glasses askew. ''Ave I left me 'ammer sumweer round your frame, Winnie?'

'I've not seen it, Dennis, 'ave you asked Mabel?'

And so it would go on, Dennis searching all round the others' frames, growing more frustrated every minute, his language becoming as colourful as he was annoyed. Then, while he was cursing his way through the weft boxes, convinced by now that someone had hidden it, I would slip it from its hiding-place and place it where he had just been searching. He would scratch his head, frowning: 'Well! Ah could've sworn . . .'

'Aye, you just 'ave!' I would grin. 'Whatever would your vicar say if 'e 'eard you goin' on like that?'

For Dennis was a verger at a local Anglican church. I played this trick several times until I found myself under suspicion whenever Dennis had genuinely mislaid his hammer, and the joke was on me.

Now, as Christmas came closer, there were rumours of several mills in the district going on short-time, some even reducing their workforces in order to cope with the worsening recession. 'Of course,' said most of my workmates, 'nothing like that will happen at Highams.' It was an old-established family firm, well-known in the area as a consistent employer. The older workers had great faith in Mr Michael and Mr William, as they called those two members of the family who still came to the mill, believing they would never allow Highams to close down. But one afternoon, just after starting work at two, we winders were called into the presence of the general manager, who told us that shift working in the winding-room was to come to an end that very weekend. We would be required to start work at half-past seven and finish at half-past four with an hour for dinner, beginning the following Monday. The part-timers who worked half-shifts would finish altogether: there was a need to economise and this was the only way it could be done.

We walked slowly back to our frames and got to work changing the pirns, filling the hoppers,* and piecing up broken ends as we

---

* Hoppers are containers attached to the winding-frames to hold the empty pirns upon which weft is wound.

digested this sudden piece of news. As the implications of the
change began to sink in, I realised that, when next term began,
I would be free to attend the classes every Monday instead of just
once a fortnight. For a few euphoric moments I was delighted.
Then the practical questions crept into my mind. When would I
do the shopping, the big wash, the main cleaning, the cooking?
Although the children helped in the house and Frank never minded
giving a hand, I liked to do things my way and these new hours
were going to make a mess of my comfortable routine, not to
mention robbing me of those treasured hours alone between
finishing work at two and the children's homecoming at four.
Another thought pushed its way into my now overcrowded head.
What about our wages? While on shifts we worked thirty-seven
and a half hours a week and were paid extra for unsocial hours.
Now we would be working forty hours and there would be no
unsocial hours allowance. In addition, we full-timers would have
to make up the production lost through the departure of the part-
timers, as the weavers would still be working shifts and would
need us to supply them with the same amount of weft to run the
automatic looms. We would end up working far harder for less
money and, as I saw it, working inconvenient hours as well. But
I knew I would have to accept the change. Even though I was in
my forties, I was the youngest full-timer in the winding-room.
None of the others had young families to consider and they would
probably welcome the chance to have all their evenings free. I
thought again of the regular evening classes and swallowed my
resentment at the management's complete disregard of whether
we would have any difficulty meeting the new conditions. Times
were not good and were likely to get worse. At least I was still
employed, which was more than the poor part-timers were. But
my old rebellious streak had been stirred and, although
circumstances meant I must accept the change, I felt discontented
and resentful.

When the new term started after Christmas, only eight of the
original class turned up. Mary was among those who had decided
not to return; she could not take to the idea of being told what
to read. The rest of us registered for the O level examination in

June, which still seemed comfortably distant during the cold, dark January evenings.

As I had expected, the new working hours meant more work for us in the winding-room. For me, they meant dashing to the shops during the dinner-hour, or cooking the evening meal when I should have been having my dinner. The big wash and the main cleaning were done at weekends, and reading and homework in the evenings when the children were out with friends or busy with their own homework. It seemed all wrong to me that one or two men could make a decision that changed the pattern of people's lives without any consultation whatever. Meanwhile, headlines announcing short-time working and redundancies in the mills of Lancashire began to appear more and more frequently in the local papers. There were reports of delegations of Lancashire Members of Parliament meeting Cabinet ministers to discuss the growing level of textile imports and the damage these were doing to our own industry. Questions on the subject were raised in the House of Commons, but jobs continued to be lost and no-one appeared to be doing anything tangible to end the situation. Whenever the subject came up at work, I would find myself in the thick of an argument as to whether the textile industry's long record of co-operation with employers and governments had been for the best. I believed that strong trade unions were necessary to fight effectively the kind of thing that was now happening to us, and would cite the miners and the power workers to prove my point. But the post-war days when cotton workers had been persuaded to return to the mills by the Government's slogan 'Britain's Bread Hangs by Lancashire's Thread' were long gone. Even so, few of Highams' employees of 1975 believed that what was happening to so many of Lancashire's mills would ever happen there.

At Easter, instead of the usual two days' statutory holiday (without pay, in accordance with the union's archaic agreement with the employers that textile workers should receive holiday pay only twice a year, at Christmas and at the start of the two-week summer holiday), we were given four extra days off, which meant a holiday lasting from Maundy Thursday until the Monday following Easter Monday — good for a rest but not for our pockets.

A couple of days before the holiday, one of the union reps asked
me if I would like to join the group from Highams who were going
to London to take part in a big demonstration against textile
imports. The demo was to be sponsored by the textile employers
and the unions; all expenses would be paid and trains laid on. We
would meet groups of textile workers from other areas of
Lancashire, and from Yorkshire and Cheshire, at a rally in Hyde
Park. From there we were to march to the Palace of Westminster,
where several well-known MPs, prominent union leaders and even
a Cabinet minister would be waiting to address us. Frank agreed
that it was a chance too good to miss, so on a cold, bright April
morning I arrived with the others from Highams at Blackburn
railway station, clutching a ticket that would ensure refreshments,
transport and admission to the hall where the speeches were to
be made.

We all crowded on to the train, everyone in holiday mood.
Doubtless some of my companions joined the trip simply to see
London, but I wanted not only the novelty of a visit to the capital
but also the chance to hear some good, rousing speeches. I was
not disappointed. Thousands of textile workers packed Hyde Park
Corner, where we were all given lapel stickers proclaiming our
mission. Little Joyce, a weaver from Number One Shed, stuck
hers over the place where she lost an eye when a shuttle flew out
of a loom and hit her, and she led our group along, pointing out
places of interest in a jolly imitation of a tourist guide. Building
workers and office staff waved cheerily from tower blocks to wish
us luck as we laughed and sang our way through the London streets.
The hall was packed to capacity for speakers including Rochdale
MP Cyril Smith, junior minister Michael Meacher, and a
succession of trade union leaders representing the various branches
of the textile industry. Most of these addressed the crowd as
'Brothers and Sisters'; all condemned the Government's policy
on importing cheap foreign textiles which was damaging our British
textile industry. One union delegate made a rousing call for the
banning of all such imports, not only because they caused
unemployment, but also because they were inferior. He cited a
case where an acquaintance of his had bought Portugese sheets,

only to have them fall apart at the first wash. After this, several such anecdotes were told by various speakers, Portugal emerging as the chief villain of the piece. So passionate were the speakers, so confident of the rightness of their cause, that an illusion of hope pervaded the hall, hope that such a strong demonstration of feeling, such sincerity of purpose, would move the Government to see our point of view and act accordingly. We returned home in a mood of quiet optimism, convinced that we had done a good day's work.

That evening's late television news showed several shots of groups of marchers trekking through the London streets. There was a repeat of an earlier interview with industrialist Lord Kearton, who gave his opinion that the march would prove to be merely a waste of shoe leather as governments never took notice of demonstrations. Oh well, I reflected, I had enjoyed the experience of seeing a little bit of London and listening to the speeches. The following week, all the marchers from Highams were given a day's pay for our trouble and, although the trip had been in the firm's interest as much as our own, the unexpected money was welcome and added spice to my memories of the day. But only a few weeks later, one of the other winders called me over to where she had just opened a parcel of sheets she had bought in the mill's shop. Inside the wrapping was a label: MADE IN PORTUGAL.

That evening I sat down and wrote a poem:

> We marched the streets of London to meet with our MPs,
> We hoped that they would listen and act upon our pleas;
> Lord Kearton said: 'It's futile — you'll just wear out
>   your shoes;
> A protest, to the Government, isn't even news.'
> We called on our employers to boycott foreign goods
> To save the mills of Lancashire and all our livelihoods;
> Then a certain mill in Harwood was seen to advertise:
> 'Sheets of finest Quality at a Very Special Price,'
> A friend of mine just bought some; she called: 'Hey,
>   look at these!'
> So much for our London march — the sheets are
>   PORTUGESE.

I slipped it in an envelope, sealed it, addressed it to the local evening paper and popped out to post it.

A couple of days later, my effort appeared in the 'Letters' column in bold, black type. Next morning it had been given pride of place on the works notice-board, and by dinner-time my popularity was at an all-time high. Even those tacklers* still living in the days when they had lorded it over the weavers had offered me, a lowly winder with whom they would not normally pass the time of day, their hands to shake. Soon it was rumoured that copies of the verse had been distributed to mills throughout the area, and that any attempts by my employers to 'victimise' me because of it would be countered by an all-out strike of mill operatives for miles around. I never learned how much truth there was in these rumours, but it seemed to me that the point of my protest had been missed. It was the importing of foreign goods by Lancashire manufacturers, who had sponsored a demonstration against that very practice, that called for action.

As it happened, no-one did victimise me and my attention was soon diverted by the coming O level exam, for it was nearly June. The exam was to take place four days after our Silver Wedding Anniversary on 5 June. Celebrations were planned: an 'Open House' for friends and relatives; a family meal at a posh hotel; a party for our eleven grandchildren − seven girls and four boys − and the time-honoured meat pies and cream cakes for my friends in the winding-room. There was going to be little time for last-minute swotting, that was for sure. In the weeks before the two big events, I walked round the winding-frame memorising quotations from *Romeo and Juliet,* verses from poems that Peter said were likely to come up on this year's paper, and passages of prose from the novels we had studied. That was the extent of my revision.

The anniversary celebrations began with a few drinks on the evening of the day itself, a Thursday. They continued on the Friday with more drinks. Saturday was our 'Open House' day, so we had

---

* 'Tackler' is the local name for a loom overlooker or mechanic, who is responsible for the maintenance of a set number of looms.

to be sociable and have more drinks. Sunday was the children's party and family outing day — yet more drinks. For moderate drinkers, Frank and I were doing well! The weather throughout the weekend was as hot and sunny as it had been on that other June day twenty-five years earlier.

Monday, the day of the exam, was also bright and sunny. I armed myself with a couple of Bic ball-points and a six-inch ruler, and made my way to the Adult Centre and the one-time laundry room where the exam was to take place. In my shoulder-bag were eight pieces of our Silver Wedding cake, one each for my fellow candidates and one for Peter who was invigilating. I cannot recall much about the exam paper, being still partly in a state of alcoholic euphoria, which seemed a good answer to any exam nerves I might otherwise have suffered. As I handed round the cake, the others stared in astonishment at my apparent lack of nerves while we waited for the dreaded moment when Peter said, 'You may begin.' When we finally started, I remember wondering briefly what I was doing there at all and what the hell I was going to write. But I did know the books and had enjoyed reading and thinking about them. Once I began to write, everything seemed to fall into place and I must have written most of the right things, for when the results came out I had passed with a Grade B.

The first few weeks after the exam, when there were no evening classes to look forward to, seemed unbelievably empty, despite the busy life I continued to lead. The tedium of my work in the mill seemed to have increased. My 'heroism' over the imported sheets had soon been forgotten and I had been relegated to my normal place in the pecking order, somewhere between the weavers, who were of a higher order, and the sweepers. With Dorothy and my new friends, I planned to take another course, possibly two, when classes began again in the autumn. Meanwhile, time hung more heavily than ever before, as I followed the usual routine of work, housework, shopping and cooking. Dennis's antics no longer seemed quite as funny as they had when there had been the classes to provide a complete change from my daily routine, and I still resented working days instead of shifts with less money and less leisure. The evening classes had, in some way, made all these things more bearable. Now, I became more and more discontented.

One afternoon in early July, the heat in the winding-room became stuffy and oppressive. The windowless room was equipped with air-conditioning devices which were obviously not working. During our unofficial tea-break, the other winders joined me in complaining about the unrelieved heat, but no-one seemed willing to approach Dennis, who was in a particularly bad mood that day. I decided to take him on myself.

''Ow d'yer expect me to do owt about t'bluddy air-conditionin' when you bluddy lot keep breykin' t'machines?' he snapped. 'Ah'm not a bluddy magician!'

'You're not even a bloody mechanic!' I retorted, and went in search of the shift manager to air my grievance.

'It's over eighty degrees outside, Winnie,' explained the shift manager. 'You can't expect it to be cooler inside than it is out.'

I walked away in disgust to where one of the union reps was drinking from a can of Vimto. His reply to my question was even more infuriating, considering that he was supposed to represent me and my workmates in such matters.

'If t'manager can't do owt, Ah don't know wot yer think Ah'll be able to do,' and he took another gulp from his can as if to indicate that the matter was closed.

Discontent filled my mind as fully as my Grandma's aspidistra had once filled her parlour window. I *would* find something better to do than working in this dump where workers were regarded as morons who neither knew nor needed to know the purpose of air-conditioning.

Just over a week later, during the July holidays, my chance came. Frank has a maddening habit of switching on the television set long before the start of the programme he wants to see. On that fateful day, he switched on in the hope of watching his beloved England cricket team win the Test Match. A documentary was showing and an interviewer was questioning a group of women who were sitting at desks copying figures from a blackboard. One of the women was saying how much she was enjoying being back at school. Then the camera focused on a group who were sitting at typewriters listening intently to an instructor. All the women interviewed were enthusiastic about their chance to learn new skills after years as housewives or as unskilled workers. They were, it transpired, on a 'TOPS' course, or Training Opportunities Scheme. The courses were available, subject to numeracy and literacy tests, to anyone who had been out of full-time education for at least three years. A training allowance was payable, plus travelling expenses, and application forms were available on request from any employment exchange.

The credits were still on the screen as I left the house and made a bee-line for the local exchange. TOPS would be my escape route from the mill with its dust, heat and threatened redundancies; from Dennis and the unrepresentative union rep, and from the patronising shift manager. As far as I was concerned, they could go and jump up.

CHAPTER THREE

CHEERIO TO T'MILL

After the holidays, I was asked to go to the local Labour Exchange to take the aptitude test for the TOPS course in shorthand and typing. Pleading 'private business', I took a couple of hours off work. The test was held in a large, bare room on the upper floor of the Exchange. It consisted of a piece of dictation, a rather stiff arithmetic test, a passage of English comprehension and the composition of a business letter. I managed to finish in the allotted time, and within a week or so I received the news that I had passed and my course would begin the following January at Accrington and Rossendale College. Escape was at hand!

I decided that, if I were to return to the classroom full-time, I really must visit the optician. I knew my sight was worsening, but the optician's reaction to my eye test gave me visions of being offered a guide dog, or at least a white stick. He was amazed that I had managed for so long without spectacles, and strong ones at that. I saw myself peering through a pair of 'jam-jar bottoms', through which my eyes, never very large, would seem almost invisible. But he assured me that he could provide me with suitable glasses, with attractive frames which would minimise the effect of the thickness of the lenses. Then, warning me to take care on the way home in the town where I had lived all my forty-odd years, he allowed me to leave. When I received my glasses, my vision became so sharp that it was some days before I could wear them to go out alone. The leaves were just beginning to turn to the warm browns and reds of autumn and I could see plainly, for the first time for years, the delicate tracery of their patterns. The children's faces, too, seemed far more vital, and I wondered at my stupidity in allowing my precious sight to deteriorate so badly when the solution was so simple, especially as my mother, as a result of an accident some years earlier, was registered as partially-sighted and could no longer read the detective novels she loved. Never mind, I told myself, better late than never; at least there would be no need to sneak sly glances at my neighbour's pad and copy her work.

This year, along with Dorothy and all, I had enrolled for two courses — English Language, taught by Peter, and The British Constitution, taught by a young grammar school teacher named Eddie: unlike Peter, he dictated copious notes, though he was very patient and would stop and answer questions at any point during the lesson. I found his subject far more interesting than I had expected, but English remained my first love. My days at t'mill were lightened by the contrast of the evening classes, the prospect of Mary's wedding in November, and the knowledge that I would leave at Christmas.

But in October my Dad, who had been unwell for some time, had to go into hospital for what we thought was a minor operation. He and Mum had been separated only once in over fifty years of married life, and then only for a few days when a more prosperous aunt had taken my mother, sister Betty and myself on a never-to-be-forgotten visit to Blackpool in the summer of 1943, the year I left school. We had stayed in a boarding-house typical of those wartime days, Betty and I sharing a room with Mum and Aunt Veron. The house was run by a man who would have passed for the Ancient Mariner. White-bearded and blue-eyed, he had the rolling gait of a sailor and assured us that he had spent most of his life at sea as a ship's cook. We never knew his name: my aunt, when out of his hearing, dubbed him 'Tanthrobobus' for reasons known only to herself. It rained almost incessantly during our holiday, but the old fellow, after giving us breakfast and setting the dinner to cook on the old-fashioned range in his kitchen-cum-living-room, would put on an old oilskin and leave the house, only reappearing after Mum and Aunt Veron had shared out the dinner among ourselves and the dozen or so other guests. There were huge iron pans of pea soup flavoured with great ham shanks; delicious fish baked in milk and butter in deep dishes; and meat and potato pies with crisp golden crusts and thick starry gravy. How he did it in those ration-bound days we neither knew nor asked: we ate gloriously and greedily, and Betty and I sat replete while Mum and Aunt Veron washed up in the vast stone sink.

But those days were long gone and Mum and Dad had lived alone together for the best part of twenty years, the last few in a cosy Council bungalow only minutes away from our house. Mum was almost blind, so Dad, since his retirement, had taken over the shopping and housework and even most of the cooking: she had become almost totally dependent on him. Now they were to be parted and both were desperately worried, he because he felt she would never manage without him, she in fear that he might not come home. Neither of them had ever been in hospital before, and the very name had for them undertones of the workhouse, in the shadow of which they had spent their youth.

Dad's illness proved more serious than we had thought, and he needed two weeks of specialist care before surgery. Mum refused to come and stay with us, so I, living nearer to her than Dick and Betty, arranged to take time off work to care for her until Dad was well enough to come home. Every morning during Dad's stay in hospital, I would go along and fetch Mum to our house as soon as the children had left for school. In the evenings my cousin Diane, a nursing sister at the hospital where Dad was a patient, would come and drive Mum and me to visit him. The bright hospital ward filled with flowers, the young smiling nurses and the pleasant, relaxed atmosphere soon dispelled the grim image of hospitals that my parents had harboured for so long. The regular evening visits became a treat for Mum, especially when she could see that Dad seemed to be getting better and would soon be home. She revelled in the drive to the hospital — 'Eeh, Ah feel just like t'Queen Muther bein' driven reawnd in a car!' — and the ride up to Dad's ward in the lift: ''Ey, Winnie, what'll 'appen if id breyks deawn? Will we 'ev to stop 'ere aw neet or will they fotch t'fire brigade to get us out?'

My wage was beginning to be missed, so once Dad was home with a home help to look after him and Mum, I returned to work. But I had only been back a week when the office girl came in with a message that fifteen-year-old Sheila had been taken ill in college on her weekly visit there from school. She was in the casualty department of Accrington Victoria Hospital: they thought she had 'flu and wanted me to collect her as soon as possible. I dashed home to leave a message for Frank and caught the next bus to the hospital, where I found Sheila lying behind a screen, pale and unrecognising.

'There's really nothing to worry about,' the duty nurse assured me, 'rest and plenty of fluids will soon put her right.'

We left the hospital in an ambulance and Sheila was violently sick all the way home. During the night she became delirious, in her clear moments complaining of unbearable head pains. In the morning I called the family doctor, who ordered her to hospital immediately, handing me a scrap of paper to give to the ward sister on arrival. I glanced at the scrawled note as he left the house: 'Suspected meningitis.' My mind was in a turmoil. Only recently the granddaughter of an acquaintance had become deaf as a result of this very illness. Valuable hours had already been wasted when Sheila could have been having the necessary treatment. Laura, then two years old, helped me control my feelings by remarking that she hoped Auntie She' would be better in time for Saturday's wedding: 'We don't want 'er bein' sick all over t'cake, do we, Gran?' And I had to laugh in spite of myself.

Hospital tests confirmed meningitis, which meant that Sheila needed a lumbar puncture. Hearing but not understanding this fearsome phrase, she begged me not to leave her. The large, fierce-looking doctor insisted that 'Mother must leave' until after the operation, but although normally deferential towards such hallowed beings as doctors, I now stood my ground and refused to leave my child unless he removed me physically. He grudgingly gave in and I held Sheila close and comforted her through the unpleasant performance. Despite its frightening onset, the form of meningitis she had contracted was a mild one. Within a day or two, she was begging to be allowed home to wear her new trouser suit to Mary's wedding. This was not to be, but Saturday evening found a bedraggled wedding party — consisting of the bride and groom, four bridesmaids and Frank and me — standing round Sheila's hospital bed. The day had been one of minor disasters. It had rained heavily and incessantly; and Mary's dress had suffered the double disaster of having the zip burst at the altar and wine spilt down its front by a nervous waitress at the reception. But Sheila was getting better and, for the moment, little else mattered.

By the time Sheila was well enough to be left alone after her return from the hospital, I expected soon to leave the mill and begin my TOPS course. But our troubles were not yet over. The week before I was to hand in my notice, Frank was made redundant. I said I would keep my job and postpone the course until he found work.

'You will bloody 'ell!' was his response. 'It might be t'last chance you'll 'ave to get out o' t'mill — we've allus managed before an' we'll manage now.'

I gave in my notice the following week as planned. The other winders were full of admiration for what they saw as my bravery in taking up such a challenge, but Dennis, predictably, had to put in his penn'orth. With his usual scintillating wit he roared, within hearing distance of all who cared to listen: 'Hey, Winnie's goin' to be a brain surgeon — oo's not circumcisin' me!' My genuinely witty Mum would have been as delighted with my retort as were those who heard it: 'If that's where thi brain is, it's time tha were circumcised!'

On 18 December, just in time for Christmas, Eileen, who a few months earlier had gone to live with her boyfriend, Billy, and his family, gave us a new granddaughter, Leanne. Frank and I had not been too pleased about her leaving home, but were delighted with this tiny replica of Eileen. I now had only four children at home, and my life had begun to change in many ways. I had always been far too busy to imagine that the day would ever come when the children's needs would not fill all my time. Starting evening classes and passing my first O level had given me, by chance, a new interest as the children grew up and began to make their own lives. I was enjoying the two O level courses I was taking, and was looking forward to the TOPS course. Although the unemployment figures were increasing, neither Frank nor I had much doubt that he would soon find work. True, he was now in his forties, but he was strong, healthy, experienced and willing. I was not unduly worried as I collected my last pay packet and said 'Cheerio to t'mill.'

CHAPTER FOUR

A NEW LIFE AND NEW AMBITIONS

Leaving the mill to go on a full-time college course at the age of forty-six was more of a venture into the unknown than I had anticipated during those last weeks of marking time at my winding-frame. I was so pleased to leave what I was getting away from at the mill that I had not given much thought to what I was going to do on the TOPS course. But now I found myself wondering more and more just what I was letting myself in for. I knew nothing about working in an office. I remembered my sister Betty taking weekly lessons in shorthand and typing, but could not recall her ever making use of whatever skills she acquired. All I knew was that, wherever I had worked, the office staff had been a separate and privileged breed, apart from the common workers. Invariably, they had started work later than we did; they had had separate cloakrooms and lavatories and, in places where such facilities were provided, separate canteens. Now that I was about to learn their skills, I began to feel uneasy and to wonder how I would cope with working in close proximity to the 'Mr Michaels' and 'Mr Williams' of this world, assuming I could get a job at the end of the course. But I pushed my misgivings to the back of my mind and turned to the practicalities, such as what I was going to wear for college in place of the overalls I had worn for work.

The TOPS course was to begin after the New Year, giving me two weeks' Christmas holiday, instead of the few days we were allowed at the mill. During the holiday, a meeting was held at the College for new TOPS students. I was relieved to see that there were one or two other women of about my age, although most were in their mid-thirties. Between thirty and forty of us attended the meeting. We were split into two groups, shorthand/typing and audio-typing, to be known as TOPS 9 and TOPS 10. The Vice-Principal of the College explained the purpose of the courses; then the Head of Business Studies went on and on about the wonderful

43

lunches served in the College dining-room by catering students. Some of the teachers outlined the structure of the courses, and I began to feel a bit more confident. What really helped, though, was the sight of two of my evening class friends; and although they would be in the other group − TOPS 10 − we could travel together and exchange notes and experiences.

Two weeks later, in the cold of a wet January morning, Sylvia, Susan and I stood shivering at the bus stop along with half the schoolchildren in Great Harwood. The 8.20 bus never came. We moved thankfully towards the next one to come along, only to be told: 'Sorry, ladies − schools only.' We finally arrived at college very wet and very late. The others made for the room where they were to report, and I tapped timidly on the door of the one where I was to have my first shorthand lesson. Miss Earley's gentle voice called me in, waved away my stammered apology, and told me to find a seat.

The lesson had already begun and the blackboard was filled with dots and strokes which apparently symbolised the letters P and B, and T and D. By the end of that first morning, I had found that being 'good at English' was not much help when trying to write 'Tow the boat to the bay' in Pitman shorthand. Eventually, I did master the shorthand to the modest speed of sixty words a minute, and I even enjoyed it. Miss Earley used to tell me I wrote beautiful shorthand; but my trouble was that I never wrote it at all − I *drew* it, and that was my downfall. While I was carefully drawing the loops and curves of the symbols, my less artistic companions were getting the dictation down on paper at the rate of ninety or a hundred words a minute, leaving me far behind.

If I thought shorthand was difficult, typing seemed impossible. Many of the other students already had some typing skill, and had joined the course merely as a refresher. 'Clump. . . clump. . . clump. . . ' went my clumsy fingers, while the smartly-dressed young girl behind me tapped away at a speed I never managed to reach. My sole distinction in the typing class was being the one whose name never appeared on the wall chart as having reached a speed of twenty words a minute with no errors. But I persevered and, at the end of the course, I passed two typing exams with credit.

As well as shorthand and typing, we had lessons in Office Practice, Commerce, Business English, Book-keeping and Business Calculations; so the timetable left us with little time to spare. I was a non-starter at Book-keeping, invariably muddling my credit column with my debit, and I fared little better with the Business Calculations. The English lessons gave me my only chance to shine, and soon both Mr Roberts, the English teacher, and Miss Earley were urging me to take A level English at the first opportunity. At the time, though, I had quite enough on my plate.

The full-time TOPS course supplied an even greater contrast to the monotony of my work in the mill than the evening classes. I was no longer an appendage to a piece of machinery, a robot to be used or cast aside at the whim of management. Here, I was an individual with a mind and with strengths and weaknesses of my own.

The winding-room seemed a world away from the old-fashioned classrooms of what had been the Boys' Grammar School, and was now part of Accrington College, where the TOPS courses were held. The hours were, if anything, more convenient than the full-time day hours that I had resented so much on the sudden change from shift working. There was little change in the domestic routine I had grown used to during my year on days. I left home forty-five minutes later than I had done then, and was home only a few minutes later than I had been from the mill, despite having to travel to and from college by bus. We were not required to do homework for the course, so I was able to keep up with my studies for the two O levels I had begun at evening classes in September. Although the TOPS course was only for six months, I was not sorry to have given up my job. Just as I had made new friends at the Adult Centre, so on TOPS 9 I soon became part of a foursome with Jean, a vicar's wife who enjoyed mild beer and beef and piccalilli sandwiches at the pub across the road; Veronica, attractive, elegant and an avowed atheist; and Alison, sophisticated and well-spoken, who loved to shock everyone as she once did by turning up minus the blonde, curly wig which we had believed was her real hair.

At home Frank was trying, not very successfully, to adapt to life on the dole. For two or three weeks, he seemed to enjoy the novelty of being a 'househusband'. He shopped, cleaned and cooked — surprising us one day with a 'Day of the Triffids' spaghetti bolognese made with half a pound of minced beef and two whole packets of long spaghetti, and another time with a delicious stew of best shin beef and fresh vegetables flavoured with a pint of best beer. After about a month, he took up the offer of a place on a three-month training scheme at a light-engineering works a couple of miles out of town. He knew that the scheme would not lead to a permanent job — skilled workers were being laid off as the trainees were being shown round — but the allowance paid was several pounds higher than his dole money, so he took it and continued his search for a 'proper' job.

In early February, we were delighted by the news that Kathleen, in Dundee, had given birth to a healthy boy, Jamie. Kathleen's first son, Andrew, had died in infancy, so Jamie gave us special reason to rejoice. A week or two later, our happiness was marred when we heard that my Dad must return to hospital for further surgery. His operation had not prevented the spread of the cancer which would soon end his life. All that could be done now was to minimise the pain.

Poor Dad could not accept that his active life was over and that there would be no more of the long country walks that had given him so much pleasure; no more sunny afternoons spent watching his favourite cricket and chatting with old friends. Cousin Diane did all she could and made sure he was physically comfortable, but my heart ached as I watched his desperate attempts to keep going in the normal way. He insisted on doing the shopping and taking the washing to the launderette as usual. One Friday teatime, riding down Church Street in Sylvia's husband's car after college, my eyes were drawn towards the figure of an old man walking slowly and painfully in the direction of the town gate. Although I could not see his face, there was something familiar about the set of his thin shoulders, from which hung a raincoat that looked several sizes too large for him. Strands of silver-grey hair had escaped from under his flat cap to straggle untidily on his collar. His trousers flapped loosely around frail legs that seemed almost incapable of supporting his meagre frame. Horrified, I realised that I was looking at my Dad. By the time we reached the gate, a kind neighbour had driven him home, but that picture of him still haunts me and overshadows happier memories of the proud, gentle, intelligent man who had loved babies and had never tired of my own children and their incessant questions.

Soon after this, Dad became housebound, but he steadfastly refused to stay in bed. Every morning Frank, now back on the dole, having finished his 'training', went along to help Dad wash, shave and dress. When he could no longer count out his prescribed number of pills, it was Frank who made sure that he took them. Each evening, he saw Dad safely into bed, and sat with him until sleep came. The evening classes lost their importance during those last few weeks of Dad's life, and I sat with Mum chatting or watching television while Frank tended Dad. In early June, just a year after joining us in our Silver Wedding celebrations, my Dad died in the little bungalow home where he and Mum had spent their last happy years together. The night before the funeral, I stayed with Mum.

'Ay, Winnie, Ah'll be fain when tomorrow's o'er wi' — but Ah'll not skrike; if there were one thing yer Dad couldn't stand it were snotherin' an' yellin' an' Ah'll not skrike at no price.' And she kept her word.

After the funeral, she lived alone in the bungalow. She now had a regular home help to do her cleaning, and the Meals on Wheels ladies brought her a cooked dinner twice a week. Barbara volunteered to get her pension and do some of the shopping, and all the children visited her as often as they could, for they had many happy memories of picnics and tea parties with Grandma when they were small. Every evening, I visited her and made sure that she had all she needed for the night. Kevin, then fifteen, spent his Saturdays with her, a custom he took over from young Frank, who had spent all his Saturdays with my parents since he was quite a small boy, keeping up the habit even when on leave, until his marriage. She came to us every Sunday, as she had done with Dad when he was alive, remaining as cheerful and uncomplaining as she had always been, much as she missed him.

The TOPS course was coming to an end along with the evening

classes. Dad's illness had caused me to miss several sessions, but
I had managed to keep up with the reading, and my surreptitious
copying-up of Dorothy's Politics notes in the Book-keeping class
– where the teacher had long since given me up – helped me
towards passing the exam. The Business English, which included
grammar, punctuation and vocabulary, made up for the English
Language classes I had missed, and I was fairly confident of a
pass in both subjects.

The week following Dad's death saw a change in our family
fortunes, for Frank started a new job as an assistant groundsman
employed by the School Playing Fields Department of Lancashire
Education Authority. The hours were 8.00am until 4.30pm, with
an occasional Saturday morning. 'School hours,' he beamed.
'Ah'm reyt 'til Ah retire an' Ah'll live to see our Frank on
t'pension.' It was indeed 'just the job' for him. As one of a team
of four, including a foreman, he travelled to schools all over the
Ribble Valley in a Lancashire County Council van, preparing
football and cricket pitches, mowing, edging, planting: exactly
the kind of work he had always yearned for. Although the pay
was not high, the job was superannuable, all holidays were paid
and there was even a sick-pay scheme. 'Isn't it funny,' I remarked,
'that you were able to be there all t'time my Dad needed you,
an' now 'e's gone you've got what you allus wanted?'

As for me, with the two O levels coming up as well as the
shorthand and typing exams, I was far too involved in practice
and revision to give more than an occasional thought to what I
would do when it all finished at the end of June. The recession
was becoming serious, and one or two TOPS students had already
left to take jobs before they were all snapped up by summer school-
leavers. I had known almost from the beginning of the course that
I was not office staff material: I would be lucky if someone took
me on as a tea lady. On reflection, I was not sure that I wanted
to work in an office at all, unless it was quite a small one with
no competition from hundred-word-a-minute perfect secretaries.
I had no regrets about joining the course. I could type after a fashion
and it had been a new and enjoyable experience, a great contrast
from working in the mill. Best of all, I had made many new friends

and become much more confident through mixing with other TOPS students from a variety of backgrounds.

The idea that I should take A level English began to seem possible. I had enjoyed the English Language evening classes every bit as much as the English Literature. Our Lady and St. Hubert's had already given me a good grounding, and Peter had given high marks for my grammar, spelling and punctuation. I had already spoken to Peter about the possibility of taking an A level English course at the Adult Centre the following year, but he felt there was little hope of attracting enough students to justify it. I made up my mind to do it somehow, even if I had to go back to the winding-frame to pay for it.

One morning, just before the end of the course, Mr Toole, our popular Commerce teacher, took us on a trip to see the main College buildings in Sandy Lane, to help us relax before our typing exam. During the coffee break, Jean, Alison, Veronica and I made our usual foursome at one of the small tables, where a young woman was sitting alone. She was friendly and talkative and explained that she was taking a full-time A level course and hoping for a job in social work. The local authority, she told us, gave her a mature student's grant: not much, but enough to get by on. As we left, Jean took my arm: 'I know what you're thinking, Winnie,' she said. 'An A level course would've suited you much better than shorthand and typing, wouldn't it?'

The rest of the term at college was hectic, for the exams had begun. During that week, I was allowed time off to take the British Constitution O level and, what with the usual routine of cooking, washing, ironing and cleaning at home, plus my nightly visits to Mum, I was kept far too busy to dwell on my new ambitions.

Summer had at last begun when we left college for the last time, with our course certificates. For the first few weeks, I wilted in the heat, glad of the chance to sit in the shade of the back garden and relax when the housework was done. Margaret had left school at about the time my course ended, and had started work in a shoe factory. Now, only Sheila, Kevin and Maureen remained at school. With the house less crowded and the children away all day, it was much easier to keep the place tidy. When people asked how many of the children were still living at home and I said, 'Only four,' eyebrows would go up. *'Only* four! I've more than enough with two' − or whatever − they would exclaim. But it does not take much imagination to realise the difference between caring for four almost independent teenagers and coping with eleven children, three of them under school age, as I had done after Maureen was born.

As the weeks went by, the novelty of being at home all day began to pall. Not only did I miss the feeling of independence that earning a wage of my own had brought; I missed, even more, the company of other women. It was difficult, not to say boring, to practise shorthand on my own with no-one to time me. The evening classes had ended for the summer break, leaving me with no homework to occupy the extra time that I had longed for, but which now seemed empty and wasted. I applied unsuccessfully for several office jobs. No-one seemed to want a middle-aged, not very competent shorthand-typist whose previous experience consisted of a six-month TOPS course. Jean wrote to report that she had had no success on the jobs market; I heard that Veronica, who had done very well on the course, taking and passing advanced typing exams, was working full-time as a machinist at Brooke Bond Oxo in Great Harwood; and Alison, who had also done well, had returned to her old job as a hotel receptionist. I began to think that Susan had been right when she said that TOPS courses and the like were a Government ploy to disguise the real numbers of unemployed. Frank's experience of 'training' had suggested this, but I had been too involved in my new life at the time to apply it to the TOPS course.

The six-week school holiday was a welcome distraction, with family picnics in the nearby countryside and day trips to the sea. When Margaret returned to work after her two weeks' holiday, and then Sheila, Kevin and Maureen went back to school, I felt more and more frustrated as my attempts to find a job came to nothing. The children seemed to grow out of their clothes and shoes more quickly than ever. I needed money: my thoughts turned back to the mill whose chimney I could see from my front door. The pay had been quite good, and Lily and the others were still there.

Dennis was there, too, of course, and would crow over my failure to become a 'brain surgeon', but I could give him as good as I'd get. Besides, I still wanted to take A level English, and the fees would be difficult to find unless I was working. One evening in August, I told Frank I intended to go across to the mill and ask for my old job back.

'Nay!' he exclaimed. 'You mean to say that after managin' to get out of it all, an' after passin' your O levels an' typin' exams an' all that, you're just goin' to give in an' go back without a struggle?'

'What d'you mean — without a struggle? What about all th'applications I've sent off an' all that callin' at JobCentre just to be told they're sorry but there's nothing suitable? At least I'll get a wage every week if I go back to t'mill, an' I'll be able to 'ave a go at an A level.'

'What about that lass you told me about — 'er that were doin' A levels at college?' he demanded. *'She* weren't workin' in t'mill to pay for 'em. Why don't you write to somebody an' see if you can do t'same as 'er? You've nowt to lose an' if they won't let you, well, t'mill'll still be there.'

When he's in that mood, it's no good arguing with Frank, so I sat down and wrote to the Principal at Sandy Lane, putting off my visit to Highams for the time being. I thought it very unlikely that I would be accepted for the full-time A level course, as I had only just finished the TOPS one. But I was offered a place, provided that the local education authority agreed. Encouraged by this, I wrote to County Hall. Feeling that perhaps I was pushing my luck, I mentioned the mature student's grant. After posting the letter, I began to have misgivings about mentioning the grant: perhaps I would be considered rather *too* mature. But the letter was already on its way, so there was nothing for it but to wait and see what happened. To my surprise, County Hall agreed to pay the grant providing the proposed course was a full-time one. I could hardly believe my luck. I wrote to Sandy Lane for the prospectus, and soon had a letter from the Vice-Principal suggesting that I take A levels in English and in British Government and Politics, with perhaps an O level to make up the required hours for a full-time course. I had been so taken up with the idea of my A level English that I had not given a thought to the other subjects. True, I had found O level British Constitution interesting and stimulating and had passed at Grade B, but I did not feel capable of an advanced course in Politics.

'Oh, Win, don't talk wet!' said Frank, impatiently. 'You'll piss it!'

And with that succinct and eloquent expression of his faith in my academic abilities ringing in my ears, I sat down to complete the enrolment forms. My spirits rose as I sealed the envelope. I was to study A level English and be paid while doing it! If I should manage to pass the Politics exam as well, that would be a bonus. If I failed, they couldn't eat me, could they? I went to sleep that night in a state of euphoria. September couldn't come too soon for me.

CHAPTER FIVE

SANDY LANE

'Please, Miss, can you tell us where Room 21a is?'

September, and my first day at Sandy Lane had arrived at last. Life in a college of further education was not a bit like I had imagined. The day had begun with a meeting of all first-year students in the College hall. The Vice-Principal had been at great pains to inform us that this was no longer a college of further education, but a 'tertiary college' which catered for people of all ages and from all walks of life. There were many more teenagers in the hall than older students, and no-one seemed anywhere near my age. Not that the age difference mattered. Ever since leaving school, I had worked with people of mixed ages, from teenagers to old-age pensioners, and had never had any problems about that. I did expect the younger students to be curious about my presence in the classrooms. After all, I was older than many of their mothers. But, once the novelty had worn off, I hoped to be accepted as just another student working for my A levels. At the end of the meeting, we were split into groups of about ten with personal tutors, mine being a pleasant woman named Mrs Clarke, who gave each of us a timetable and a list of room numbers where our various teachers were to be found, and sent us off to enrol for the courses we hoped to take.

Now, for what seemed the umpteenth time, I had been mistaken for a teacher by a group of young girls and boys who looked as lost and bewildered as I felt after tramping countless identical corridors, looking for the enrolment rooms for A level English, British Government and Politics, and O level Social and Economic History.

'Sorry, love,' I said, 'I don't know where I'm supposed to be going, either!'

On the TOPS course, we had been told which rooms to go to for classes, and I had not realised that there would be so many

53

students doing so many different things at this college that everyone
would have to find their own way.

At last I managed to sort myself out and went to meet Linda,
my new friend, for a cup of tea in the refectory before the afternoon
meeting for all students in the College gym. Linda was about the
same age as my eldest daughter Mary and, next to me, the oldest
member of Mrs Clarke's tutor group. She had introduced herself
before we separated to find the enrolment rooms, confiding shyly
that she felt worlds apart from the teenage students, a confession
which came as no surprise to me, as my own older children often
seemed to have come from a different planet compared with their
younger brothers and sisters. Linda, in her early twenties, was,
in some respects, closer to me in my late forties than she was to
students less than ten years younger than herself. The self-assured,
almost arrogant manner of many of the younger students towards
the teachers was a far cry from the respect both Linda and I had
been brought up to show towards our 'betters'. Despite my
increased confidence, my ingrained habit of deference towards
teachers was extremely difficult to exorcise. Nevertheless, my
growing awareness of my own attitudes went a long way towards
helping to change them and, while I was never as nonchalant as
some of my young classmates, I certainly no longer believed that
teachers, by virtue of their position, were superior beings.

The meeting in the gym that afternoon proved the point. The
head of PE, who evidently saw himself as a High Priest of Health
and Fitness, sternly declared that *all* students were expected to
take part in some form of physical education. Those who
contemplated breaking the sacred rules of his gymnastic temple
would be subject to unnamed disciplinary measures which would
make them very sorry indeed to have incurred his displeasure.
I sat there, shoeless, and vowed that this was the first and last
time I would set foot in the place. My vow was strengthened when
a hapless girl in front of me let out a nervous giggle and was treated
to a scathing diatribe which, if anything, made this little man even
smaller in my eyes. I resolved that my PE would consist of nothing
more than the daily dash to the bus stop and the climb up Sandy
Lane.

Next day, classes began and I soon grew used to the routine laid down by my timetable. The hours were similar to those on the TOPS course, except that there were occasional free periods between classes which could be spent in the library or chatting with friends. Wednesday afternoons were given over to something called Liberal Studies − which, I was told, included PE − but I left college at dinner-time and my Liberal Studies consisted of washing, cooking and cleaning! Linda was in my English group and another classmate was Julia, a widow and mother of a teenage family. Our set play was Shakespeare's *King Lear*. It had not entered my head that I might see the play as well as read it, but I was in for a treat. During the first term, there was a mid-week outing − unheard-of for a mill worker − to see Donald Sinden in the title role at Stratford. I liked him on television, and I liked him even better on stage. Before that, my only visits to the theatre had been for Christmas pantomimes. I had fallen in love with Shakespeare when I first read *Romeo and Juliet* and we had done those drawings of the Globe Theatre at evening classes, so it was even more exciting to be going to see my first serious play in his birthplace. I know it sounds daft, but I had thought that going *to* college meant staying *in* college, and here I was going all the way to Stratford in a minibus with a gang of teenagers when everybody else was at work!

We also studied First World War poets, so Frank's knowledge of the War was not just interesting but useful. At first, Chaucer's *Franklin's Prologue and Tale* was as strange to me as Shakespeare had been that first evening at the Adult Centre, and I relied a lot on the glossary at the back of the book until I discovered Neville Coghill's bawdy translation. A level Government and Politics was an anti-climax at first, hardly any different from O level British Constitution. Later, it became more interesting when we studied political behaviour, voting patterns, and political systems other than our own. I became more selective in my choice of newspapers and television programmes, though I still enjoyed an occasional half-hour catching up with the goings-on in Coronation Street, and continued to follow faithfully the adventures of Marlon, Wellington, Maisie and the rest of the Perishers in the *Daily Mirror*.

My experiences of both working and family life had left me with few illusions about the fairness of our society, and academic study gave me no reason to change my views. If anything, it made me more convinced of the way in which the system stayed much the same as it had always been, with the rich getting richer and the poor getting just enough to keep them quiet.

Often, when the older children came to our house, there would be lively discussions on current trade union issues, the merits — or otherwise — of the monarchy, the state of British industry, and any other topics that came to mind. The younger members of the family were never backward in coming forward: Margaret was now seventeen and a worker herself; Sheila and Kevin were sixteen and fifteen respectively; and Maureen was an argumentative thirteen-year-old. Although all of them were articulate and not afraid to express their views, the younger ones seemed much better informed than their older brothers and sisters had been at a similar age, probably thanks to radio, television and the modern teaching methods which had given them a wider view of the world than the earlier, more rigid education system. Their knowledge of the 'three Rs' may be much less thorough, but they had far more self-confidence and awareness of life than I had at their age. They were, as my Mum would put it, 'fit to travel'.

Mum herself, though she said little, was tickled pink, I knew, by my having made it to college. When an inquisitive neighbour asked, tartly, 'How's your Winnie getten to t'College?' Mum retorted, 'On t'Corporation bus, Ah fancy.' My mother had a great sense of humour which Dad had shared, though his was inclined to be rather dry. They loved to bandy words with each other, Dad often admitting ruefully that 'It takes a good mon to get at t'back o' thi mam!' He had done it once, and was not allowed to forget it in a hurry. A few days before his seventieth birthday, Mum asked what he would like as a present. 'Two minutes' silence'll be awreyt,' said Dad, quietly.

During those warm summer evenings after his death, when I made my regular visits to see that Mum was all right and to settle her in for the night, I would find her sitting on the bench outside the bungalows, entertaining the neighbours with stories of her past. She had a talent for making the most mundane happenings sound hilariously funny, and had a splendid memory for detail. The children loved to visit Grandma and listen to her tales of the old days when she had been a half-timer in the mill at the age of twelve, leaving school a year later to work as a weaver from six in the morning until six in the evening. She could recall when times were so bad locally that she and several of her contemporaries had had to get up at 4.00am to walk to a mill miles from Great Harwood, to run two looms each for a few pence more than they were paid on the dole. One of her companions, having had one of her looms stopped for part of the week, had earned so little on that occasion that she dropped behind as they walked home and flung herself into the canal where she drowned rather than face her mother with her meagre wage.

'It used to be eight o'clock at night when we got home; I've fa'en asleep mony a time over me tea,' Mum told us.

But she preferred not to dwell on the hard times. Instead, she stressed the fun they had had in the days of hobble skirts and wide-brimmed hats with 'foller-me lads' streaming behind for the young men to snatch at on the Sunday promenades along Whalley Road, where many life-long romances began. Mum was one of a large family, and her mother, my Grandma Whittam, was a real martinet. When they were young, my mother told me, if she or her sisters spoke out of turn they were in big trouble.

'Eeh, she'd get 'old of yer 'air as you were goin' out o' t'door an' give you such a slap across t'face wi' a wet dishcloth. Eeh, it didn't 'alf 'urt!'

One evening, just after ten, as Mum and three of her sisters were walking home together from a church social, they neared their house to see Grandma, arms folded, waiting grimly at the gate.

'There's no daycent folk out at this time!' she called, when she saw them.

Aunt Nelly, still full of the enjoyment of the outing, retorted smartly, 'Well, get in, then.' And all four of them were kept in for a month as punishment. If ever we children went to see her on our own, she would look at us over her specs: 'What're you after?' I don't know why she asked, because she never gave us anything.

Mum had known long hours and hard times in the mill as a girl, but she loved to tell of the good times she remembered. One of her favourite memories was of the Christmas tradition of the Village Wedding, when all the workers, irrespective of their place in the pecking order, had dressed up to perform a mock marriage ceremony. It was usual for a tall, lanky tackler to play the part of the bride, with a small plump woman as the groom. Being only four feet ten, almost as broad as she was long, and with a jolly, rosy face, Mum made an ideal groom, a part she revelled in. Walking arm-in-arm with her sheepish bride and followed by a motley procession of guests and attendants dressed in all manner of comic finery, she must have been in her element, for she loved to play the entertainer. And here she was, a widow after more than fifty years of marriage, missing Dad only she knew how much, and still entertaining others and making them laugh.

Joining my Mum and her friends on those evenings and listening to their reminiscences of far-off days appealed to my sense of history, though it was far removed from the flag-waving propaganda taught during my schooldays under the name of History. So it came as a shock when I joined the Social History O level class at college to find that times I had lived through were part of the syllabus: the Second World War, the birth of the Welfare State, the coming of television to the mass audience, and the 1944 Education Act which identified me as a relic of the elementary school system, and one of the last generation to have left school at fourteen. I had not minded when Sheila, my only adult classmate, had been grateful to see 'an *older* face', but I had not bargained on being regarded as a bit of history myself.

I found the History course absorbing, for, again, it was not History as I had known it, but a subject relating to real people and their lives. The teacher was a gloomy-looking individual with a sharp line in barbed comments, mostly concerning the deplorable attitude of modern youth towards work. He was very knowledgeable about his subject and generous with well-illustrated handouts, so long as you were punctual in attending his classes. Woe betide those who were even a minute or so late: the handouts would be withheld and the offenders left to manage as well as they could. My age did not excuse me from this treatment — which was fair enough — but on the credit side, he did give praise where it was due, and I was no exception for that, either.

As in the English O level classes, I did quite well with my course work in the subject at A level. The Politics essays were not quite so easy. Although I usually received a fairly good mark for my written work, I had to work harder for it than I did in English. But I held my own with the teenage members of the class. Frank was very supportive and would listen patiently as I read my essays aloud for his comments and criticisms, boring though they must have been to him. Occasionally, our political discussions developed into full-blooded arguments, when the academic theories in my essays contrasted with the common-sense views formed from his experience. His knowing that, for the most part, I shared his political opinions, feeling more strongly than he did on many issues, made it difficult for him to understand why I wrote as I did.

'Look, Frank, I have to be objective,' I pointed out during one of our arguments. 'The examiners are not going to be interested in what *I* think — they'll be looking to see 'ow much of Mr Fallon's lectures've got through to me, or at least 'ow much I remember of 'em.'

'Well, it seems a bit of a waste o'time to me if you can only write what you're told. I mean, it sounds OK when you read it out — you can put it down all right; it's just that when it comes to 'ey lads 'ey, there's nowt in it of any substance.'

'Listen, will you? I'm not writing what I'm told as such. I'm answering the question at the top o' the paper, an' it leaves no leeway for puttin' personal opinions. I'm studying Politics as an academic subject, which is different from giving my own political views.'

'All right, Win. I suppose you know what you're doin'. I'm no scholar an' I've never pretended to be.'

These arguments with Frank kept my feet on the ground and, though I enjoyed studying Politics, I remained at heart the same woman who had been so outraged by the Portugese sheets.

As I had hoped, the teenage students soon grew used to my presence in the classrooms, and I became quite friendly with several of them. Sometimes, as I walked up Sandy Lane or sat sharing the coffee break with a group of young friends, I would wonder what I was doing there instead of tending my winding-frame at Highams Premier Mill. I even felt vaguely guilty, for it seemed wrong in some unaccountable way for me to be receiving money for having chosen to study rather than working manually for it as I had always done until now. Then, one day, Margaret came home from work with a grim expression on her normally cheerful face.

'What's up, Margaret? Something wrong at work?' I asked, as I brewed her a cup of tea. She shook her head slowly, then changed her mind and nodded.

'I wasn't going to say anything to you − but I were that mad! I don't know why some folk can't just mind their own damned business!'

'Well, what's to do, then? Has somebody been interferin' with your work or summat?'

Some of Margaret's workmates were quite a lot older than she was and had worked at the factory for years. One or two of them had convinced themselves that no-one could run the machines as quickly and efficiently as they, and especially not someone young, like Margaret and, therefore, much less experienced in the work. More than once she had complained about the condescending and even, occasionally, catty attitudes towards her of some of these older women. My advice to her was that they were best ignored.

'Just do your work and take no notice of 'em; they're probably scared that you can do more than them seein' as you're so much younger and fitter than they are.'

But now she explained: 'Oh, no. It's nothing to do with me work, Mum. It's just that somebody asked how you were getting on, an' when I said you were doing your A levels and went to college full-time, one of 'em started going on about how it were a bit off − you going to college an' me working in t'factory.' She stopped to gulp down a mouthful of tea. 'Anyway, she got what she asked for! I give her a right mouthful! I told her that you've done your share of hard work if you never do another stroke. An' I told her that you and me Dad've allus worked to keep us lot, and now we're working and paying taxes, and if you've got brains to go to college, well, good luck to you and it's nowt to do wi' anybody else.'

'And what did she say to that?' I was full of gratitude and admiration for my daughter's spirited defence of my decision to go to college.

'Well, what could she say? It's true, isn't it? We're not asking *her* for anything. Anyway, t'others said I'd just done right and she'd asked for it.' And Margaret, cheerful once more, tucked into her tea with her usual healthy appetite. Then she added, grinning, 'I'd hate it at college, anyway — all t'teachers at St. Disgustin's were glad to see t'back o' me! I don't know how you stick it, Mum, all that reading an' writing. I'd rather be working where I am now — even if I have to put up wi' a nosey old bitch like her!'

Margaret's unconscious suggestion that study and hard work are unrelated to each other made me smile, but she was right that what I chose to do was no-one's business but my own. Subconsciously, I had worried about what other people might think about me studying at college while my daughter was doing the kind of factory work that I had rejected. But I knew what she thought, and I also knew that, should the occasion arise, she, too, would have the courage to change the direction of her life. Young as she was, she had helped me to get my priorities right, and I made up my mind that, from now on, I was going to enjoy myself while I had the chance.

Taken as a whole, there was a good deal of difference between this course and TOPS. For one thing, all the TOPS students had been over twenty-one. On the A level course, the comparatively few adult students were working alongside youngsters from the high schools and comprehensives who were well-versed in the techniques of passing exams — not just the odd one or two, but often as many as ten or more within a space of two or three weeks. Most of them were full of self-assurance, which spurred me to greater efforts to keep up with them and hang on to my own bit of new-found confidence.

Just before the first term ended, internal exams were held and

I was relieved to learn, when the results came out, that I had done very well in English and, although, in Mr Fallon's words, I 'hadn't broken any pots' in Government and Politics, I had not disgraced myself.

On 24 November 1976, whilst I was sitting the first part of my Politics exam, a more exciting event was taking place a few miles away in Rossendale General Hospital. Two events, to be precise, for our daughter Anne, who now lived in Waterfoot, and daughter-in-law Jean gave birth within an hour of each other to Daniel and Christopher respectively. Three days later, Heather, our seventeenth grandchild, was born to Mary and John.

My life outside the home had changed a great deal during that first year after leaving the mill, but family life remained much the same. Although I naturally had much more homework than I had had for the evening classes, I did try not to let my studies interfere too much with our normal routines. Sunday was still very much a family day shared with Mum and, quite often, one or two of our married children with husband or wife and their children.

The five-minute journey to our house was as much as Mum could comfortably manage by then, with her poor eyesight and failing health. This meant that, though we loved to have her, we were tied to the house on many fine Sundays when we might have been visiting Frank's mother in Clitheroe, or Anne and Michael and their families in Waterfoot; or just going for a walk in the surrounding countryside.

'I'll 'ave to get a car,' Frank declared.

After a series of intensive driving lessons, he passed his test first time, and for £150, plus tax and insurance, we found a comfy old Zephyr which was just what we wanted.* It was early March, just the right time of year to buy a car, with all summer before us in which to enjoy the new freedom it would bring.

Sadly, the car lasted longer than my dear Mum. We had only one Sunday afternoon drive with her, and her second and last outing in the car was to the maternity ward of Queen's Park Hospital,

---

* Our total weekly income at the time was in the region of £70, out of which we paid about £22 in rent and rates as well as the usual household bills and everyday living expenses.

Blackburn, where young Frank's son, also named Frank, was born on 21 March 1977. A few days later, Mum tripped and fell, banging her head on the corner of the old-fashioned sideboard that stood in her living-room. For a week she lay in the double bed that she and Dad had shared, looking small and white-faced, the ugly bruise on her forehead a sharp contrast to the pallor of her normally rosy complexion. It was Easter week and I was on holiday from college, so I stayed at the bungalow, dozing on Mum's settee during the long nights, and spending the days brewing the endless cups of tea she asked for, though she could only manage the merest sip. Visitors came and went: her sisters, children, grandchildren, friends and neighbours. For much of the time she was in a world of her own, where she saw her parents, or Dad.

'Your Dad's been this afternoon; Ah towd 'im to give o'er moitherin', Ah'm awreyt an' Ah'm bein' looked after.'

One day she 'saw' my brother Arnold, aged six or seven, I guessed, for he was 'all in white, bless 'im, stood theer as good as gowd all afternoon.' The only time boys wore white when we were children was as first communicants, or on May Sunday for the church procession. Once they left the infants' classrooms for the Boys' School at the age of seven, they wore their Sunday suits for walking day. During her lucid moments, Mum was as jolly as ever. She teased Diane and Mary, who came daily to wash her and make her comfortable: 'Yo' two − you've allus wanted to get me wheer yo' thowt yo' could keep me quiet. Well, you've getten me, but I'll not be quiet. Mind what yer doin' − me ear 'oyl's full o' sooap − yer after weshin' me away, t'pair on yer, but Ah'll show yer!' As soon as she saw Dick it was 'Eeh, Dick, Ah could just do wi' a drop o' brandy to put in me tay. Tha'll get thi Mam a drop o' brandy to mek me 'air curl worn't ta?' When the young parish priest expressed his shocked sympathy at her condition, she teased him, too: 'Ay, Father, Ah'm not so bad, yer want to see t'other mon!'

After tea on Good Friday, I sat by her bed and noticed that a little colour had returned to her cheeks. All day she had lain quietly, her breathing becoming more laboured as the hours passed. As I sat there beside her, she suddenly spoke: 'Ay, tha's bin a good

lass fer thi Mam, Winnie. It's me birthday next week an' Ah want
'em all to coom − all t'chilther an' me brothers an' sisters an'
everybody.' During the night, she died and, just a few hours later,
Frank and I drove to Haslingden Register Office with David and
Carole to witness their marriage, arranged weeks earlier. After
the wedding, the four of us went straight home. We had planned
a quiet meal out, but no-one felt like celebrating. On 14 April 1977,
her eighty-fourth birthday, we buried Mum in the grave where
we had buried Dad less than a year earlier. I remembered her
standing there, dignified and determined, keeping her vow not to
'skrike at no price'. She is still an inspiration to me, this brave
and cheerful little lady who had possessed few of the material things
of life, who had worked hard since childhood, had brought up
a family during the hungry 'thirties, had lost a much-loved son
and could still say, having been left alone and almost blind, 'Eeh,
aren't I a lucky woman?'

I returned to college to face the summer exams feeling very much
the orphan I had so suddenly become. Yet it was difficult to remain
unhappy for long thinking of my Mum. She had always been so
jolly, and I knew she would hate me to be sad, so I told myself
how lucky we had been to have her for so long, and set my mind
to the task of passing the exams.

The long summer holidays were here − nearly three months during
which I planned to set aside time for study each day, to become
so familiar with the texts of *King Lear* and *The Franklin's Tale*
that I might have written them myself; and to read the 'quality'
papers and keep well ahead with the current affairs programmes
on radio and television, so that I would be as 'politically aware'
as even Mr Fallon could desire when the second year began and
A levels proper were in view. By now, you see, I felt I owed it
to myself to achieve a reasonable pass in the Politics A level; and
to Mr Fallon, too, whose dictation speed would have done credit
to Miss Earley, and who must have had an almighty thirst after
a double lesson on Friday afternoons. And to the family who had
patiently sat through *Question Time*, *Weekend World*, *Panorama*
and so on, while I made frantic attempts to scribble down the

relevant points made by commentators and politicians on the
burning issues of the day.

Perhaps I became a little too 'politically aware' for my own good.
June 1977 was the month of the Queen's Silver Jubilee. One or
two letters appeared in the local evening paper condemning
members of a left-wing group who had vandalised decorations put
up in Blackburn in honour of the occasion. I agreed with the writers
that the vandalism was mindless, but not that objectors to the cost
of the celebrations should keep their opinions to themselves. Ever
a champion of free speech, and believing that the huge amount
of money in question could have been put to better use, I put my
thoughts on paper and sent them to the Editor.* Immediately it
appeared in print, my letter was construed by fervent Royalists
as an unwarranted attack on the Queen, though I had been at pains
to emphasise that my main object was to support the principle of
free speech. Evening after evening, letters appeared deploring my
'anti-Royalist' views. I was lectured on my good fortune in living
in a country where opinions such as mine were permitted to be
aired. One irate reader offered to start a fund to send me to Russia
'where there is no monarchy and no free Press'. The true point
of my letter was ignored; I held a minority view concerning the
Royal Family and my critics were blind to all but that fact. In vain
I protested that my real purpose was to point out the value of
freedom of speech, and that they were the ones who apparently
wished to suppress it. When a woman from my own home town
had a scathing letter printed suggesting that, as a council house
tenant and mother of a large family to boot, I had no business
holding opinions, let alone expressing them in public, I decided
to leave my critics to their views. Opposition to my opinions,
however ill-informed, was one thing; personal vindictiveness from
a woman I had been acquainted with for most of my life and who
had never given any indication of such feelings towards me was
quite another. It worried me more than a little, for my letters,
though strongly worded, were without malice and, while I knew
that they were bound to arouse strong feelings, I had expected

* See Appendix D.

an impersonal response. Frank, as usual, summed up the episode
in his matter-of-fact way: 'Look, cock, she's just a stupid woman
who can't see any further than 'er own nose, an' it upsets 'er to
see somebody like you who can.' The private support I received
from people in the street and unpublished letters from readers of
the paper made me wonder whether public free speech really
existed in Britain.

But the fuss blew over and, meanwhile, more pleasant
happenings were taking place within the family. During that same
June, Carole and David had a son, David, on Jubilee Day itself,
which qualified him to receive a special mug as a memento of his
auspicious birth date, and caused much family amusement at the
irony of it all. In July, while Kevin spent a few days with Jean
and Michael and little Robert, Frank and I, with Sheila and
Maureen, drove up to Dundee to see Kathleen, Andy and Jamie,
stopping off at Barbara's mother's home near Dunfermline to drop
Margaret and two friends whom Mrs Philp had offered to put up
for a week's holiday.

What with all this coming and going, and visits to and from our
married children living nearer home, the summer flew by and it
was plain that I would return to college for my second year only
slightly more familiar with the contents of my textbooks than I
had been at the beginning of the holidays in June.

Sheila had left school at the end of the summer term and, when
Kevin and Maureen returned to their lessons in mid-August, was
still searching, without much hope, for a job of some kind.
Unemployment had continued to increase, particularly in the North,
and more and more school-leavers were joining the dole queues.
One dinner-time, Margaret came home with the news that there
was a temporary job available for Sheila in the shoe factory. Sheila,
bored with hanging round the house and sick of having little or
no money to spend, jumped at the offer. She already had a place
on a junior secretarial course starting at college in September, but
insisted that this was her second choice. She would go to college
rather than remain unemployed; but, if a permanent job came up,
no matter what it was, she would take it.

'But you've a chance of a good job later if you take this college
course,' I pointed out.

'If a job turns up and I don't take it, I might not get another chance, qualifications or not, t'way things are going. I want a job now, then I know I've got one.'

I thought of my own youth and of how I had been able to walk out of one job and straight into another with the minimum of fuss. True, they had all been dead-end jobs, but all I had wanted was to be working and earning a wage. That was all I had been brought up to expect. Today's young people were urged to work hard at school, where their lives were ruled by the need to pass exams. They were told that success in these was essential if they hoped to do anything other than unskilled work. These days, you needed O levels to be a tea lady. Sheila had passed her CSE exams with good grades, and I felt that she would enjoy college life and do well on the secretarial course. I hoped she would discover that she did not like factory work, and would opt for college after all.

It was not that I objected to factory work as such. Goodness knows, I had been glad enough of it myself when I needed the money it brought me. But my own experience had shown me that people are too often judged on the basis of the kind of work they do, rather than for what they are. It was partly because of that attitude towards working people that I had been prompted to leave the mill, so I was surprised that Sheila was proposing to turn down a college place for the first factory job that turned up.

In the end she had her way, for the temporary job became a permanent one: 'You've no need to worry, Mum, I'm OK at work an' I like it. Us young 'uns aren't like you lot were, you know: nobody'll put on *me*.'

Like her older brothers and sisters, Sheila had made her choice and seemed happy with it. As she had pointed out, they were not at all like 'us lot' had been at their age. Whatever their occupations, most of the young people I knew, including my own children, had a sense of their own value as individuals that 'us lot' had never had.

CHAPTER SIX

NEW BABIES AND NEW ASPIRATIONS

That September, when we started the first term of our second year at college, all the students were very aware that they now had to get down to work, and the atmosphere was no longer as free and easy as it had been.

There were few jobs and fewer apprenticeships, so many youngsters hoped to go on to higher education and needed to pass their A levels in June. One by one they began to take odd days off to attend interviews at various polytechnics and universities. They would come back with unnerving descriptions of stern-faced dons firing rapid questions about the various subjects they were studying, and the lucky ones with offers of a place provided they achieved certain grades in the exams.

As for me, I had not really thought about the future, though I hoped vaguely that I might find a niche in adult education where I could help others to enjoy learning as much as I did. I knew of teachers who had qualified to be trained with four or five O levels, and I saw no reason why three A levels should not take me on to such a course. But that had been a few years earlier, and I soon discovered that a university degree was a normal requirement for the teaching profession. In spite of having broken away from the mill, passed exams and gone to college, I was still very much the working-class product of Our Lady and St. Hubert's Roman Catholic Elementary School, and still more than a little surprised, when I thought about it, at my boldness in coming as far as I had. Apart from the College staff and Peter and Eddie of the evening classes, I had met few graduates and, of those, as far as I knew, only one came from a working-class family. A few years older than Frank, this young man had passed his eleven-plus and gone from grammar school to Cambridge — where he gained an excellent science degree, but lost all trace of his Lancashire accent, which seemed to me rather a pity. On the other hand, my course work marks were as good as, and in some cases better than, those of many of my younger classmates. It was only three years since passing a single O level had seemed beyond me, and the idea of a university education had never entered my head. I didn't even know what a don was!

Now I had already passed four O levels with good grades,* and the more I thought about the idea of going on to university, the more I liked it. Not only would it improve my chances of eventually working in adult education, but it would mean another three years being paid to enjoy studying English. I sent off for information on degree courses to the three universities within reasonable travelling distance of home, and decided to apply for a place.

Some of my classmates already had definite plans for their futures. Julia, who had nursing experience, had been offered a place on a training course for tutors at a local teaching hospital. Linda hoped for a degree in primary education. The three of us had become friendly with a group of women from the Rossendale Valley who, like us, were studying at A level. They all seemed very articulate and well educated, especially Stella, who became my firm friend. She spoke so well and had such self-confidence that I did not think she needed further education. She told me she had been to art school, trained as a dancer, and later toured with a professional theatre company. Her childhood, in the Midlands, had been spent in an atmosphere of good books and pictures, there had been regular visits to concerts and theatres, and she had travelled abroad quite a lot. Her background was a complete contrast to mine, yet we soon found ourselves chatting away like old friends.

Like Julia and Linda, the Rossendale group had already planned their next step while I was still dithering over whether or not to apply for a university place. They had none of the doubts that I nursed, and had simply completed and sent off application forms, and were already going to interviews with Doctor This and Professor That at various institutions. But events at home took

* My four O levels were English Literature (grade B), English Language (grade A), British Constitution (grade B), Economic and Social History (grade B).

my mind off any thoughts of my academic future. Margaret, by now a plump and pretty eighteen-year-old, began to suffer violent bouts of morning sickness.

It was a golden morning in early October when I heard the unmistakeable sounds coming from the bathroom. She loved her food, but I had not worried when she started eating less, because I thought she was simply slimming to be fashionable and that her appetite would overcome her vanity before she starved. Now I listened with increasing dismay, for, as far as I knew, Margaret had no steady boyfriend, being far too fun-loving and happy-go-lucky to get involved in a serious relationship − or so I had believed. She flew downstairs and out through the front door with her usual 'See you tonight, Mum!' before I had a chance to question her. All that day, I went through the motions of my college routine, preoccupied with thoughts of Margaret: what I would say to her (what *could* I say to her?); what Frank would say when he knew what had happened; who the father might be; and whether just possibly I might be wrong.

Poor Margaret! The minute I spoke that evening I knew I had been right. No, there wasn't a special boyfriend − not really. It was just a boy she liked rather a lot, and she'd thought he felt the same way about her. Yes, she'd told him and, no, he didn't propose to do anything about it. As a matter of fact, he'd gone off to work abroad as soon as he heard the news, and in view of his attitude she hoped never to see him again, so there was no point in telling me who he was, was there?

She was right, of course, though I doubted if Frank would see it that way. I thought of the hullaballoo we had had when he found out that Mary was pregnant with Laura soon after Anne had married just in time for Andrea's birth. The idea that a daughter of his should be taken in by someone without the guts to face up to the consequences of his actions was anathema to him and would, I knew, make him really angry. But I also knew that, once he had let off steam, he would let the matter rest, and that when the baby arrived he would be the one to spoil it, be it boy or girl.

I was right about the row. It was an almighty one, of which the less said the better. I was also right about the aftermath. No amount of questioning would make Margaret tell us who the father was and, after simmering for a day or two, Frank settled down to the idea of having a baby in the house again, and, for the time being, our domestic life returned to normal.

It may be that Margaret's baby was the catalyst that helped me make up my mind about what I was to do after A levels. The baby was expected in May, just before the exams were due to begin. Margaret was strong and healthy and planned to work until mid-March, then return to her job after maternity leave. That meant that, if all went well, she would return to work in November, for she was determined to keep her baby herself and maintain her independence. But who was to take care of the child while Margaret was at work? I wanted to help her in every way possible, but my youngest was now fourteen and, if I was honest, I knew that to be tied to the house with a young baby was not what I wanted for myself. Much as I loved babies, I now wanted to continue my studies. I wanted to know more about the English language and to explore more of English literature. I wanted to be surrounded by books and learning and to spend my time reading and writing, listening and discussing. I wanted to go on meeting people and making new friends. Yet I wanted also to retain my own identity and stay among the people I had always known, in the place where I had my roots. I wanted very badly to have my cake and eat it.

I need not have worried. Margaret had already decided that her child would go to the local day nursery and mix with children of the same age.

'I know you'd look after it well, Mum, but you've got your own life, an' I don't see why you should change all your plans to look after my baby. Besides, if it stays with you all day an' you're doin' everything for it, it might think you're its mum an' I'm its big sister, an' I don't want that to happen.'

The prospect, then, of being stuck at home with another baby had made me realise how very much I wanted to go on to university, and Frank said, 'If that's what you want to do, Win, you go on an' 'ave a do, an' good luck to you!'

All three of the universities within daily travelling distance of home were difficult to reach on public transport from Great

Harwood. Before joining the TOPS course, I had always worked within walking distance of home, and catching buses every day had been as novel to me as the course itself. By now, of course, I had become quite a seasoned commuter between Great Harwood and Accrington, but the thought of a daily journey to Manchester was more than a little daunting. I could count on my fingers the number of times I had visited Manchester (twenty-odd miles away) in the whole of my life.

Manchester and Lancaster Universities each offered a Single Honours course in English leading to a BA degree. Preston Polytechnic offered combined courses, and the University of Salford, a Joint Honours in Arts and Social Sciences. I decided to apply for Single Honours in English as a first choice and, if I could not do that, to try Salford, where I could study English and History with Politics for the Joint Honours. With only a day or so to go before the deadline date, I posted the completed forms and settled down to prepare for Christmas which, with two whole weeks' holiday and no young children at home, was going to be an easier task than I had been used to. It was our first Christmas without both my Mum and Dad, and I was expecting it to be tinged with sadness, especially as Dad's birthday came just a few days before. Although I knew that Mum would have disapproved of such a 'waste of money' with a few well-chosen words — for she believed in 'flowers for the living' — I bought a holly wreath to put on their grave, feeling that, in spite of her disapproval, she would have appreciated my motives, just as she had always appreciated the bunch of spring flowers I gave her each year on our Arnold's birthday. As I put on my coat to take the wreath to the cemetery, young Frank arrived.

'I'll come with you, Mum,' he said, then, teasing me for my absent-mindedness: 'You'll probably put it on t'wrong grave if you go by yourself!'

I was grateful for his company, and our visit to the grave became an annual Christmas ritual. Afterwards we would go back to our house to drink hot coffee and reminisce about past Christmases with his Grandma and Grandad so that, for a short while, they seemed close again and I felt cheered by the happy memories and comforted by my son's understanding.

Christmas Day itself was as jolly as it had ever been, despite my morbid expectations. Although we no longer had small children in the house, and the teenagers who remained with us now chose their own presents — fashion clothes and such — just for old times' sake I wrapped each of them a small gift from 'Father Christmas' to be opened on Christmas Day. After breakfast, Frank and I visited as many of our grandchildren as we could, to share their Christmas fun. Barbara, being from Scotland and far away from her family, joined us with young Frank and their two little daughters for Christmas dinner. Later, while we sat chatting and watching television, David, Mary and John dropped in for a Christmas drink.

'Remember last Christmas, Mum, when I took Grandma down to our house for a glass o' sherry before dinner, an' she supped nearly 'alf a bottle? Eeh, she didn't 'alf enjoy it!' grinned David.

'Ooh, yes,' cried Mary, 'an' what about when she used to ask for a fag an' we all used to sit round 'er an' watch 'er do t'swallow! She only did it at Christmas, an' then only for a laugh.'

'Yes an' if any of *us* lit up she used to nearly break 'er neck lookin' up at us, an' say "You'll not grow if you smoke, you know," an' we were all 'ead an' shoulders taller than 'er!'

'An' Grandad 'ud sit there wi' 'is pipe, chucklin' away to 'imself.'

CHAPTER SEVEN

HIGHER INSTITUTIONS

When the new term started, we were kept hard at work preparing for the 'mock' A level exams in February. My Politics group had an exciting time to look forward to immediately they were over, for we were off with Mr Fallon on a trip to London and the Houses of Parliament. The group, which consisted of myself and six teenagers, four girls and two boys, were to travel down to London in a mini-bus driven by our tutor on the first Wednesday in March. We had booked rooms in a small, cheap hotel near Earl's Court, and arrangements had been made for us to be shown round the Houses of Parliament on Thursday morning and to attend Prime Minister's Question Time in the afternoon, followed by tea with our local Member of Parliament. Wednesday and Thursday evenings would be ours to do as we liked, and we were looking forward to visiting the theatre and doing a little shopping before returning on Friday afternoon. To my young classmates, used to Continental holidays and weekend shopping trips to Preston and Manchester, the trip was a good excuse to be away from lessons for a couple of days. To me, it was something altogether more exciting.

But before this special outing, I had an interview for a place on the Joint Honours degree course at Salford. Before coming to college I had not known that there *was* a University of Salford. I had a vague idea that Salford was a suburb of Manchester, somewhere near the Granada television studio where *Coronation Street* was filmed. I had heard of Lowry, the Salford artist of 'Matchstick Men' fame, and I knew that Walter Greenwood's *Love on the Dole* had been set in the Salford area. As an eleven-year-old I had knelt before the Bishop of Salford to be confirmed, but Salford itself was merely a place I had heard of, no more than that.

Frank took a day's holiday to drive me to the University for my appointment with the senior course tutor. It was a raw, grey day in late February, the route was unfamiliar and we were late in arriving. I was a little apprehensive at the thought of meeting one of these interrogator dons, and said nervously to Frank, 'Ooh, I 'ope 'e doesn't start askin' me all sorts o' clever questions that I can't answer − I'll feel a right idiot if 'e does.'

'Whyever should 'e do that? 'E knows what subjects you're takin', so 'e's not goin' to ask you about summat you know nowt about, is 'e?' answered Frank, reasonably. 'Anyway, I daresay there's plenty o' things you know that 'e doesn't.'

'Mmm, I suppose you're right − 'e'll know nowt about windin' an' weavin' for a start, nor 'ow to make a good potato pie for thirteen folk!'

I found Colin Harrison not at all like the inquisitor I had expected. Brushing aside my apology for arriving late, he began to question me the moment I stepped inside his room. But his questions had little to do with the topics I was studying. He was far more interested in my background and family, what Frank did for a living, our children and grandchildren; and about my work in the mill before I had left it for the TOPS course. He seemed genuinely impressed by the fact that I had passed my first O level after thirty-odd years away from the classroom and, apart from one or two general queries, seemed not particularly interested in my A level subjects. Finally, he shook my hand warmly, thanked me for coming and told me that the University would be offering me a place conditional on my passing both English and Politics at grade C. General Studies, which I was also taking, could be ignored.

''E was smashin'!' I reported, joining Frank for a quick cup of tea before we set off on the journey home. ''E 'ardly asked me anythin' about th'A levels − 'e were more interested in *me* than in what I were doin'.'

'I told you it 'ud be awright − you moither too much, Win, that's your trouble.'

The mock exams proved quite difficult, and it was a relief to hand in the last paper and forget about them until our return from London. I felt a twinge of regret that Frank was not coming on the trip, but it was not strong enough to prevent me from looking forward to it with almost childlike anticipation. I had left plenty of easy-to-prepare food in the house and knew that I could rely on Margaret, now visibly and happily pregnant, to ensure that no-one starved in my absence.

Apart from the textile imports demo, I had visited London once before, but only for a day, to visit Earl's Court when young Frank was in the Navy and a member of the Portsmouth Field Gun Crew taking part in the Royal Tournament. It had been a wonderful occasion, but there had been no time for sight-seeing that day, so I was determined to make up for it on this trip. I had a little chuckle to myself when a senior member of the College staff offered her good wishes for an interesting few days: 'Such a relief to have a responsible adult accompanying the young people, especially the girls, on a trip like this.' The 'young people', I knew, were far more seasoned travellers than I was, but I smiled politely and kept that knowledge to myself.

We arrived in London in the late afternoon, parked the mini-bus in a convenient spot and caught a bus to Earl's Court, where we soon found our 'hotel'. It was one of a long row of Georgian terraced houses which had clearly seen better days. The front steps and soap and water had been strangers to each other for a very long time, and I reflected that a good scrub and a going-over with a Lancashire donkey stone would not come amiss. The milk bottles on the doorstep were unwashed, and there was putrid and unmistakeable evidence of a visit by a stray dog which made me apprehensive about the inside of the place. But we pressed the bell bravely, to be admitted by the surly proprietor, who collected our money, produced the register for us to sign, handed us the keys to our rooms and, after pointing us in the direction of a narrow staircase, disappeared into his cubby-hole of an office.

I was to share a room with Lois, my particular friend in the group. We had two reasonably clean single beds, a cracked wash-basin and an old double wardrobe, which were all we needed as we had no plans to spend any of our precious waking time in there. Returning to our room after a visit to what passed for a bathroom, I came across an apparition in the form of a thin young girl wearing a kind of night shirt, who seemed to gaze through me unseeing before vanishing up the stairs to the next floor. Lois and I agreed that we would be safer using the cracked wash-basin in our room, an impression confirmed when we overheard a rough, male, Cockney voice telephoning for an ambulance because 'the stupid bitch has gone an' taken anuvver bleedin' overdose'.

My life had not been so sheltered that I had never heard of the 'drug scene', and I knew that, even in small towns like ours, there were drug addicts. But witnessing this scene was a chilling experience, made all the more disturbing by the callous indifference in the man's tone. I thought of my own daughters, and especially of Margaret and the pregnancy that had caused me so much anxiety when I had first suspected it. The old Lancashire saying that 'You can 'ave a lot worse things than babies' came to mind, and I felt thankful that Margaret was so much more fortunate than the poor girl upstairs.

Apart from the hotel, London was all that I had anticipated and more. I don't mean to give the impression that the people of the small towns of Lancashire scarcely ever venture more than a few miles from home. Without eleven children and two full-time jobs, many families can and do. But for me at that time, the trip to London was an adventure to look forward to and to savour to the full. The pure pleasure of visiting the theatre to see live on stage the shows that are normally mere adverts in the Sunday papers; the thrill of riding through the brightly-lit, still bustling streets after midnight in a real London taxi-cab where half a dozen people can sit facing each other; the exhilarating experience of sitting in a café eating 'junk food' that I would never have looked at at home, watching through the window a colourful and seemingly endless procession of people of many nationalities, and knowing that, after the meal, my friends and I would be part of it. As I window-shopped with Lois, I found myself thinking of my own teenage daughters and how they would have enjoyed all this. Maureen was not quite fifteen and still at school, and I knew she would have loved it. Margaret and Sheila had chosen to work in a factory, but it seemed unfair that they should be missing so much while I was sharing it with other people's daughters. I thought of my Mum and Dad, and wondered what they would have had to say about their Winnie going to London to visit Parliament and listen to 'all them spoutin' politicians'.

On the Thursday morning, we were shown round the Houses of Parliament by an elderly gentleman who had spent all of his working life as a Parliamentary messenger: he knew every nook and cranny of the place and a great deal of its history, which he explained in a way that brought it all to life. We were searched several times during our tour, and again in the afternoon as we entered the Commons to take our seats in the Strangers' Gallery. After listening to all the lectures about the workings of Parliament and the time-honoured traditions and protocol of the House of Commons itself, I felt a strange sensation as I peered down at the rows of green leather seats and realised that I was actually inside the building where, for generations, the major decisions of State had been taken.

Question Time itself was a bit of a let-down. The questions were dull and the answers non-committal. After the first few moments, my attention began to wander because it was much more entertaining to spot the well-known faces that appeared regularly in the newspapers and on television. Margaret Thatcher looked younger than I had imagined, fiddling with the buttons of her neat blue suit; Helene Hayman, looking more like a student than I did, swept in with her young baby in her arms; Enoch Powell was apparently enjoying a snooze — and who could blame him? There were a few sharp exchanges between the occupants of the Front Benches, with opposing choruses of 'hear, hear!' and 'shame, shame!' from the back-benchers. When Michael Foot likened Norman Tebbit to a 'semi-house-trained pole cat', a commotion comparable to a Saturday football crowd almost drowned the high-pitched calls of Speaker George Thomas for *'Order!'* All the while our 'honourable' representatives strolled casually in and out of the Chamber as if it were their local pub or a working men's club, places where even I had seen more serious political debate.

At 3.15 the Prime Minister, James Callaghan, rose to answer questions 'requiring an oral answer', and I made a conscious effort to concentrate on what I hoped would be some worthwhile Parliamentary exchanges. I need not have bothered. The Prime

Minister was required to answer thirty-three questions in all. Fourteen separate MPs rose during the allotted fifteen minutes or so 'To ask the Prime Minister, if he will list his official engagements on Thursday 2nd March'. Eight times the Premier was asked to state his plans for official visits to places ranging from Chelsea in London to Salisbury in Rhodesia. There were four inquiries as to 'when he last met the Confederation of British Industry'; three identical ones about the Trades Union Congress (and one about meeting both the CBI and the TUC). After two questions asking for details of the Opposition response to his 'invitation to discuss immigration', the last one called for a 'statement on the progress in implementing the proposals in the Gracious Speech'. So much for Parliamentary democracy, I thought. The whole affair was patently designed to ensure that no-one was required, or even enabled in the given time, to offer any information of the slightest value. Most of the questions were constructed in such a way as to embarrass either the Premier or the Opposition Leader, neither of whom seemed in the least perturbed. I was not surprised that so many MPs were opposed to the televising of Parliament: the wonder was that they allowed members of the public into the place at all.

We returned to college the following week to face the results of the mock exams. I had a Grade A in English and was bordering on a B in Politics, which gave me the confidence to accept invitations for interviews at Manchester and Lancaster Universities, for although I had been offered a place on the Joint Honours course at Salford, I still felt I would prefer Single Honours English.

I set out for Manchester on a wet, blustery morning in mid-March. My appointment was in the afternoon, but I was not sure where the University was, so I felt it wise to go early and give myself plenty of time. When I arrived in Manchester, the rain had stopped and the weather had become warm and sunny. The streets were crowded and, by the time I arrived in the English Faculty carrying my raincoat on my arm, I was hot and red-faced and my feet felt as heavy as lead in my knee-length, fleecy-lined winter boots.

My two interviewers had little in common with the kindly Colin
Harrison of Salford. The questions came thick and fast, all
academic and each more difficult to answer than the last. When
they had finished, one of them, glancing at his copy of my
application form, cleared his throat in an affected manner and
remarked: 'I see you have no formal modern language qualification,
Mrs Bridges.'

'No, I'm afraid not; I *have* listed all my qualifications and my
potential ones on the form.'

'It would be very difficult for you to follow a Single Honours
English course without some knowledge of a modern European
language. Haven't you studied French or German or any language
other than English at some time?'

I began to feel as if these men were deliberately trying to
embarrass me for some obscure reason of their own.

'I've already told you that *all* the relevant information is on the
form,' I pointed out. 'You must have known I haven't done a
modern language before you asked me to come for interview.'

'Not necessarily,' smiled his colleague. 'You might have taken
a course in Conversational French or something like that, though
it wouldn't really be much use for entry to an English degree course
— I suppose you might try for O level French this summer if you're
really set on taking English here.'

Before I could think of a suitable reply to this suggestion, his
friend chipped in: 'There *is* an alternative, you know. What about
taking a combined course in, say, Social Studies and some other
discipline with English as a minor subject? You would then drop
English after the first year, and there would be no requirement
for you to take the Anglo-Saxon section of the course, so you
wouldn't need to bother about a modern language.'

'Sorry,' I said, picking up my things. 'If you'd read my
application properly, you'd have seen that I've specifically chosen
to do English as my first two choices. Obviously, if your prospectus
had made it clear that a modern language O level was a requirement
of the course, I needn't have wasted my time coming here. Good
afternoon.'

With as much dignity as I could manage, I left for the long

journey home. Well, I reflected, if those two were typical examples of university dons, I was not impressed, nor would I be in awe of any others I was likely to meet in the future.

I arrived back in Great Harwood feeling dejected at the thought of Frank's disappointment when he heard how I had fared. During the journey home, I had decided that there was no point in going to Lancaster to be interviewed as they would doubtless require O level French or German or something before accepting me for an Honours degree in English. As I passed Highams, I found myself coming near to regretting having left what was, admittedly, a boring job, but was at least an uncomplicated means of earning a living.

Frank listened sympathetically to my tale, his expression growing more indignant with every word I spoke.

'I tell you, Frank, I got t'feelin' they'd only asked me to go so's they could 'ave a look at a middle-aged 'ousewife 'oo'd left school at fourteen an' fancied 'erself as an intellectual.'

'Bloody toffee-nosed snobs, that's all they are!' he railed. 'I just wish I'd 'a' bin there − they'd 'ave learnt a modern language awright, an' a bit o' bloody Anglo-Saxon an' all! Sod 'em, cock! Get to Lancaster or Salford an' show them snotty buggers at Manchester what they're missin' − they want bloody French for an English degree!'

I went to bed comforted.

Although, as it turned out, there was no need for a foreign language qualification at Lancaster, and after my interview there I was offered a place conditional on two B grades, I had already set my heart on going to Salford, an easier journey by public transport and the friendliest of the three possibilities. I even began to picture myself as a university student travelling on the express bus whenever I saw it pass by.

But when the results were published, my day-dreams came to an abrupt halt: I had achieved an A grade in English, and passed General Studies, but gained only an O level pass in Government and Politics.

The weeks preceding the exams had been hectic on both fronts. Margaret's baby daughter, Gemma Louise, was born on 9 May and soon took over the entire household. On the 25th, the exams started and Eileen had her second baby, Billy. I was kept busy revising, helping with Gemma and visiting the maternity ward. In the middle of all this, Mary, who had been fighting a form of depression since Heather's birth, was admitted to hospital, so I felt obliged to take my turn with Sheila, her mother-in-law, to help care for the children. Nevertheless, I had been fairly confident that I would pass the Politics exam, as I had studied consistently and achieved satisfactory marks throughout the year. The course tutor, Mr Fallon, was most concerned and persuaded me, against my better judgement, to have the papers checked, for I was sure that the examining board were unlikely to have made a mistake. I was right, but by now I had set my heart on continuing my studies, so I applied to re-sit in November and went back to my revision notes determined to succeed. I owed it to Frank and the family; to Mr Fallon and all those who had helped me at college; but, most of all, I owed it to myself, for I was the one who had done all the work. I had not made it to Salford that year, but I intended to get there next.

Off on a pre-war outing with Mum, Grandma Whittam, aunts, cousins and friends.
Betty and Winnie are in the front on the left.

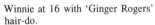

Winnie, Mary and Frank at
Blackpool, summer 1953.

Winnie at 16 with 'Ginger Rogers'
hair-do.

Frank with the cup he won at the British Legion Horticultural Show, 1967.

Young Frank, 1982.

Mary, 1987.

David, 1987.

Anne, 1986.

Michael, 1987.

Kathleen, 1987.

Margaret, 1987.

Eileen, 1987.

Sheila, 1987.

Kevin, 1987.

Maureen, 1987.

Mrs Seed, 1984 (courtesy *Lancashire Evening Telegraph*).

Gemma, aged about six months, who 'helped to make up my mind about life after A levels'.

Mum and Dad's Golden Wedding, 1974.

Winnie and Frank, 1986.

CHAPTER EIGHT

'THE WINTER OF DISCONTENT'

I was not the only one to be disappointed by the A level results. Lois had also failed Politics, but she already planned to stay at college for a further year to take English. She would be joining me for the Politics re-sit in November. I was more concerned about Julia, who had achieved only an O level pass in English and so had failed to qualify for the nursing tutor's course that she wanted to take. It had been very difficult for her, I knew, coping single-handed with five adolescents and running a home for them, as well as keeping up with the A level course work. The tutor's course was a paid one, with an almost certain promise of a secure job at the end of it. She came over to see me one afternoon and we had a long talk about it all. As I walked home after seeing her safely on her bus, I felt that although my disappointment was strong, my failure was not as significant as hers. Julia had gone home smiling after our talk, grateful for my sympathetic ear and my words of encouragement, insisting that I had helped her see the situation in perspective, and that she would now be able to come to terms with it.

But it was I who had needed to see things in their proper light. Unlike Julia, I had the love and security of a husband to help me through what, after all, was a blow to my ego as much as anything else. Typically, Frank had refused point-blank to consider that my failure could be blamed on anything I had, or had not, done.

'There must 'a' bin a mistake or else it's a bloody twist,' he insisted comfortingly, even when the examining board's scrutiny had confirmed my poor result.

I was touched to find that my fellow-students, my TOPs friends and my friends from the O level classes were as baffled by it as my college tutors. It showed their faith in my academic ability. But the fact remained that I had failed, would have to wait for more than a year for my university place, and would need to

improve my performance when I took the re-sit before I could
be sure of that. Colin Harrison wrote to congratulate me on my
English result and to offer commiserations over the Politics: if
I gained only a grade E in the re-sit, he assured me, I would be
accepted for a place on the Joint Honours course next year. People
I met in the street congratulated me on my success, having seen
my name in the lists of exam results published in the local paper,
and not realising the significance of the small letters in which 'govt.'
was printed next to my name. Though they were offered kindly,
their congratulations made me feel even worse. But, compared
with Julia, I had little to complain of, for she and her children
depended upon her ability to earn. Unlike me, who had
done it merely because I wanted to, she had taken the A level course
in order to qualify for the nursing course. She had previously
worked for several years as an auxiliary nurse gaining experience
which, in effect, made her a better nurse than many of her less-
experienced, but professionally qualified, superiors. At the
beginning of the second year at college, she had been interviewed
for the tutor's course along with more than a hundred applicants,
and was one of the few chosen as suitable for a place. Since then,
a new training officer had been appointed and he insisted on formal
educational qualifications in preference to practical experience,
so Julia's failure to gain an English A level had lost her her place.

But the following June, at her wedding to a young man she had
met on her return to her old job in a local hospital, she was
philosophical about it: 'I might never have met Derek if I'd gone
on that course,' she told me. 'It was all for the best after all, Win.'

I was delighted to see her so happy. Derek seemed a very nice
man and they were clearly very much in love. I knew that Julia
would not have taken such a serious step unless she was very sure
that it was right for her and for her family. But I secretly wondered
if a ready-made teenage family would not prove too much of a
handful for a former bachelor like Derek, and whether Julia's
widowhood and consequent need for the self-reliance which had
now become a habit would not cause difficulties when the need
arose to make joint decisions. When, some time later, Julia told
me that she was on a social workers' course and hoped to qualify

soon, I knew that she and Derek were right for each other, for he was giving her the kind of essential support that Frank has never failed to give me.

Through the summer, I really 'got my head down' on Politics revision, and determined that this time I would pass. After the November re-sit, Lois and I compared notes and agreed that this paper had been easier than the June one, and felt that we had both given a fairly good account of ourselves. But it was not until January, when the results were announced, that I was able to relax. I had passed with a grade D. I had hoped to do better than that, but who cared? At last I was certain of a place at Salford. I was invited once again to visit the University to see Colin Harrison, who made me an unconditional offer, explaining that this was a legal undertaking that I would be given a place in October. It was agreed that I would study Sociology with Psychology; English; and History with Politics. At the end of the first year, I would drop one subject and carry on with the remaining two for the degree of Bachelor of Arts with Joint Honours in Arts and Social Sciences.

'Didn't I tell you you'd get there in th'end?' beamed Frank. 'If everybody 'ad their rights, you'd 'ave bin there awready!'

Home life was going through a difficult patch just then. During the summer, Mary had been discharged from hospital and had taken a room at the hospital for the mentally subnormal where she worked. Her husband John was working in Germany, and Laura and Heather were living with his mother where the family had made their home since she had become a widow two or three years earlier. Laura was at school and Heather at the day nursery, with Sheila, John's mother, caring for them in the evenings and me helping out at weekends. Mary visited the children regularly and they seemed quite happy with the situation, though we all hoped that, when John returned to England, he and Mary would come to some more satisfactory and permanent arrangement.

Just after Christmas, the snow began to fall, lightly at first, then more heavily until all of the British Isles was covered. Many roads became impassable, delaying deliveries to the shops. There were power failures and water pipes froze and then burst. The year 1979 began with the lorry drivers going on strike over the EEC ruling that limited the number of hours they could legally drive. Goods deliveries were further disrupted: there was a shortage of petrol at the pumps and of oil to heat public buildings. Several schools closed because of the need to save fuel and Maureen, along with her classmates, was given an unofficial holiday. Kevin had left school the previous Easter and had started work in a shoe factory. Many of his fellow school-leavers had not found jobs at all and, though he did not particularly like the work, he got on well with his workmates, received a regular weekly wage and preferred it to the idea of life on the dole.

As the days went by, the weather became colder and the shortages grew worse. Shops and supermarkets began to ration such goods as sugar and cooking fats, and there were appeals to shoppers not to buy more food than they needed, so that workers who were unable to shop during the day could get their share. Public transport services became even more unreliable because of the continuing oil shortage, and I began to feel relieved that my degree course and the need to travel to Salford every day had been postponed. Each morning, I trudged through the snow to shop for the family and for some of the old people living near us, including my Aunt Teresa, my mother's sister, who was in her eighties and still as sharp as a needle. During the second week in January, David's wife Carole had a baby boy and, on their return from hospital, I lent a hand with her chores and shopped for them, too. With my three young workers coming home for a snack each midday, the usual household tasks to be done, the extra shopping and so on, along with looking after Laura and Heather every Saturday, my days were only slightly less busy than they had been when the children were all living at home.

As I shopped I listened to the comments of other working-class housewives, some of whom talked as if having to drink sugarless tea was the height of hardship. Most of them blamed the lorry drivers for the 'crisis', with remarks such as '. . . greedy . . . ought to think themselves lucky to be in work at all . . . no thought for anybody else . . .'

'Things'll never get any better for workin' folk while their own kind take this line,' I said to young Frank during one of our chats.

'I know, Mum, some o' t'lads at work are t'same, an' if you side wi' t'lorry drivers you're classed as a member o' t'loony left, as they call it. They believe everything they see on t'news an' in t'*Sun,* an' they look at me like *I'm* daft when I say only them that's involved in t'strike really know what it's about.'

'Aye, well,' I said, 'it's not 'til something affects us personally that most of us even start to think about it, Frank. Nobody ever gives a thought to t'lorry drivers when they're workin' normally an' t'shops are full o' food an' stuff, do they? You should know — look what it were like for you power workers in '74.'

'Eeh, aye! We were only workin' to rule an' I were scared o' comin' 'ome in me Electricity Board jacket — there were that many tales about power workers' families bein' victimised. We 'eard from some o' t'other areas that lads were 'avin' to take their wives outside their own districts to do t'shoppin' 'cause local shopkeepers wouldn't serve 'em.'

'Yes, well, I suppose it's same now for some o' t'lorry drivers — probably worse seein' as they're gettin' blamed for all t'shortages. Folk are entitled to their opinions, but it's a poor do when little children an' their mothers 'ave to suffer for what their dads are doin', whether or not you agree wi' em.'

'Aye, you're right, Mum, but some of our lads seem to 'ave forgotten that. Younger end are bad enough, but you want to 'ear some o' th'older 'uns! One of 'em were goin' on t'other day as if we're livin' in a workers' Paradise. "You youngsters don't know you're born," 'e says. "I can remember when I left school an' there were nowt for none of us. Me mam an' dad were both out o' work an' on t'Means Test, an' they fetched some kind of a rule in so's me mam couldn't claim on 'er own — me dad 'ad to claim for 'er, an' it were ten bob 'e got for 'er. Thirty-odd bob we 'ad to live on, an' there were four younger than me — there were none o' this Family Allowance an' Social Security in them days. We'd to make a do wi' what we got an' be thankful, but then, folk were a lot more neighbourly then; we all mucked in an' 'elped one another." It were no good talking to 'im, Mum, 'e's convinced that anybody 'oo backs lorry drivers must be a Commie or worse!'

'Yes, well, 'e's right about one thing, Frank. Folk *were* more neighbourly an' they *did* 'elp each other durin' t'bad times. I were only a little girl when your Grandad were on t'Means Test, but I can remember 'ow upset your Grandma was when me an' your Aunty Betty an' Uncle Arnold 'ad to go to free dinners instead o' comin' 'ome at dinner-time. An' I can remember what it were like an' all, 'avin' to walk up town wi' all t'other free dinner children. Eeh, I 'ated it: It were up at Mount Zion in th'old church 'all, right up t'other end o' town an' we all used to 'ave to walk up together, an' I were sure everybody knew we were goin' to t'free dinners. They 'ad long tables an' you 'ad to go an' get your dinner from a woman 'oo stood be'ind a counter. It didn't matter what they gave us, it all tasted same to me. They gave us spoons to eat with − they must've thought workin'-class children wouldn't know 'ow to use a knife an' fork − an' I can remember I once went an' asked for a big spoon instead of a little 'un. I were only about six or seven at time an' t'woman said, "What does a little girl like you want with a big spoon?" an' I told 'er because I didn't like their dinners an' I could get rid of 'em faster wi' a big spoon. You should've seen 'er face! But I can remember old Mrs Parkinson across t'road comin' wi' t'remains of 'er Sunday joint wi' most o't'meat left on it so's Grandma could make us a pan o' stewed potatoes. (Mr Parkinson were a tackler or summat, and got kept on for maintenance work when t'mill were closed, so 'e were still earnin'.) An' if anybody were ill, somebody 'ud make sure they were looked after an' t'children got a meal, no matter 'ow 'ard-up they were themselves. It was a lot different then. Nearly everybody was out o' work in these parts, as your old workmate says, there *was* no State 'elp apart from t'Means Test, so people relied on each other for 'elp durin' times of unemployment. But too many of us forget that what benefits there are 'ave 'ad to be fought for. Nowadays, even though there is a lot of unemployment an' it's still risin', there're more people in work than out of it, an' them that're in it are so busy tryin' to 'ang on to it an' keep up their livin' standards, they don't think about their fellow workers until we get what media likes to call a crisis 'cause o' somebody takin' industrial action to protect their rights; an' that's why *people*'ll 'ave to change before anything else changes.'

'Aye, I know that's true, Mum, but I don't think there's much chance of it ever 'appening. They'll forget all about this lot when things get back to normal.'

Things never did get back to normal. Prime Minister Callaghan denied there was a crisis, and refused to declare a state of emergency. But the majority of people did believe in the 'crisis' that had turned into 'the winter of discontent'. It's a pity James Callaghan didn't pay more attention to what the people thought, because later that year he was voted out of power and Mrs Thatcher in.

The snow lasted throughout January and well into February, which saw an end to the lorry drivers' strike, but marked the beginning of industrial action by the hospital ancillary workers. Some foods were still hard to get in the shops, and the public continued to grumble. Now they had the hospital workers to criticise and, when the public service workers began a series of one-day strikes, followed by the threat of industrial action by ambulancemen, feelings began to run very high.

Then David Walder, Conservative MP for the Clitheroe constituency, to which Great Harwood belonged, died suddenly. The resulting by-election would be the last to take place before the General Election in May, and was regarded as the barometer which would indicate the colour of the next Government. The media spotlight turned on Clitheroe. As the date of the by-election − March − drew near, the big guns of the political parties began to appear in our streets. Jovial Cyril Smith waddled and joked his way round the shops, Denis Healey twinkled through the main street, and Margaret Thatcher stopped the traffic on her way to patronise our small Friday market and the folk who turned out to see her. Several times I saw well-known political figures waiting outside Highams to catch the workers on their way out.

One evening, I went to a meeting in support of the new Labour candidate, Lindsay Sutton. The fact that the speaker, Barbara Castle − prominent both locally and nationally as Blackburn's MP and a one-time member of Harold Wilson's Cabinet − attracted only a small audience made it plain that Labour's support had dwindled in Great Harwood. The young and articulate Lindsay Sutton spoke as passionately as Mrs Castle (though less stylishly). Clitheroe was a Tory stronghold and, though he was clearly an able and sincere candidate, he would need a safer seat than this one to make his debut in the House of Commons — where, no doubt, he would soon be relieved of his sincerity.

As expected by most people, the Conservatives won the by-election with a substantial majority, and Great Harwood settled back into its normal state of comfortable obscurity. Two months later, Mrs Thatcher's Tory party won the General Election. Aunt Theresa was disgusted: 'If workin' folk think they'll be looked after wi' a woman like yon bossin' everybody about they're in for a reyt shock. To give 'er t'job o' runnin' t'country an' t'state it's in awready, they must be livin' in Fairyland, that's all I can say!'

But most local people still felt that 'whoever gets in, we'll still 'ave to work for our livin'.' They little realised how few of them *would* be working by the time the next General Election came round.

I had begun to look for a part-time job myself, without much success. We had had to part with the old Zephyr when she failed the MoT test, because the cost of the necessary repairs to bring her up to standard amounted to more than she was worth, moneywise, though to us she had been worth her weight in gold for convenience and the happy trips we had enjoyed in her. With Margaret, Sheila and Kevin now contributing to household expenses, it was less necessary for me to work in order to pay the bills, but we did miss the old car and our weekend trips. If I could earn enough money for a deposit on a replacement during the next few months, while I was waiting to start my degree course, so much the better. Besides, I was beginning to get bored at home all day. With the disappearance of the snow and the coming of warmer weather, the old people were again able to do their own shopping, as they preferred to. Margaret, Sheila and Kevin needed only a snack at midday, as we still had our main meal in the evening. They could quite easily get this for themselves, or take sandwiches to work. With Gemma's birth and the return of nappies to the wash-basket, we had invested in an automatic washing machine to replace the old twin tub and its faulty spin drier, so washing was no problem. Our four teenagers were quite capable of ironing their own clothes, and even preferred to: apparently the denim jeans uniform of the young required an ironing technique which my education in the art of laundering had not included.

I still looked after Laura and Heather on Saturdays, but that had become part of the normal routine, and they and little Gemma enjoyed each other's company. It would be quite easy for me to fit in a few hours of part-time work if I could get it.

I carefully searched the classified columns in the *Lancashire Evening Telegraph* and the *Harwood Advertiser,* and read the notices displayed in the JobCentre whenever I went into the town. It was here that, one morning, I found exactly what I was looking for:

> *Temporary Part-time Office Worker Required*
> Three months' employment in a local office for a general clerical worker. The work involves filing, some typing and reception duties. A pleasant telephone manner is essential. For details of pay, hours, etc., ask at the desk.

I asked at the desk. The girl on duty looked down her nose at me. 'You need five O levels for that one,' she said in a flat voice.

'It doesn't say anything about O levels on your notice.'

'Well, you need five,' she repeated, looking at me as if it were a foregone conclusion that no-one as ancient as me could possibly have taken O levels.

'Oh, I've only got four.' I paused for a moment before wiping the smug smile off her face. 'But I've got three A levels if they're any good.'

She stared at me, scarlet-faced, then rose from her chair. 'Oh, well, in that case I'll get someone to see you.'

The supervisor who emerged from the inner office was very polite. She explained that the job was temporary, with a view to permanency for the right person. The firm would not want to pay the rate demanded by my A level qualifications, particularly on a temporary basis.

'It seems a bit dishonest to advertise it as temporary if what they really want is permanent help,' I told her. 'Why don't they at least make it clear that there's a chance of permanent work for someone suitable?'

'Well, you see, if they keep anyone on for longer than three months, they're legally required to offer permanent employment. This way, if an applicant proves unsuitable they can get rid of them at the end of the three months without a fuss being made, as the job is taken on as a temporary one, anyway. On the other hand, if the applicant turns out to be just right for the job, the firm can offer permanent employment at the end of the three-months' trial period.'

'I see. Thank you for explaining. I still think it's a bit off, though. I can understand an employer wanting to protect his interests. That's perfectly natural. But this way he gets all the protection, and the employee gets none. He could find any amount of excuses to get rid of a 'temporary' worker, however competent that worker happened to be, just because he'd taken a dislike to her. But she'd have no come-back if she found out later that someone else was doing her job.'

'Yes, well, I suppose that's one way of looking at it, but I'm afraid it's the law at present.' She picked up a pen and looked at the pad in front of her. 'Now. Would you like me to take some particulars of the kind of work you're looking for?'

I explained that I was just looking for something to tide me over for a few months, and that I would be happy to take any kind of part-time work, regardless of my A level qualifications. 'Office work, shop work, factory work, or anything'll be OK. I just want to earn some money while I'm waiting to go to university.'

She promised to do her best to help, and I left to get on with the shopping.

A few days later, I saw an advert in the *Harwood Advertiser* for temporary packers at Brooke Bond Oxo, where I had worked for a time during my teens. I applied immediately, completed a form that was extraordinarily detailed, given the type of work they were offering, and was told I could start work the following day. I had not mentioned to Frank that I was looking for work, so as not to disappoint him if I didn't get any; but that evening when he came home I told him: 'We should 'ave enough for a deposit on a car by t'July 'olidays.'

'You what? 'Ow are we goin' to manage that?'

'I've got meself a part-time job at th'Oxo. It's only for twelve weeks − nine to three every day. I can do me shoppin' on t'way 'ome, an' be in in plenty o' time to get tea. It's just the job to keep me goin', an' if I save me wage every week, we'll 'ave our deposit just in nice time for th' 'olidays.'

He gave me a smacking kiss.

'Eeh, Win, you're a good lass. You think o' somewhere you've allus wanted to go, an' I'll take you for a right good day out durin' th' 'olidays, I promise!'

I was in for something of a surprise when I started my new job at the Oxo works the following morning. In my teenage days there, the management had been very strict, and I had often found myself in trouble with one or other of the supervisors for talking or for sharing a joke with my workmates. I had expected things to be more or less the same, but times had changed. No longer did stern-faced supervisors prowl the shop-floor, waiting to pounce on anyone who stopped working for a minute. The present supervisors, promoted from the ranks of the workers, were pleasant and helpful. Some of them had worked alongside me in the old days and stayed the course. They explained patiently to me and the other new starters what was required of us, then left us to get on with it, returning occasionally to check if we were managing all right.

The workroom was large, airy and well-lit. Most of it was taken up by the cube-making machines, and the remaining space contained tables where we 'temps' worked in groups of three. Just off the main room was a rest room, where we could take an occasional ten-minute break, to sit or smoke a cigarette. Further along was the women's washroom, with its long row of spotlessly clean lavatories opposite a line of washbasins, each with its own large mirror. There was scented soap and an electric hand-dryer. The walls were tiled from floor to ceiling in pale turquoise. All in all, it was a far cry from the squalid facilities provided for manual workers by most other firms I had worked for. The subsidised canteen contained pool tables, dartboards and a telephone for workers' use. Even in my day, there had been a trained nurse in attendance in the first-aid room, but this had now been extended to include a small room with a bed, where a sick worker could rest while waiting to be taken home.

Re-packing Oxo cubes that had been returned to the factory because they were wrongly packed was monotonous but clean work, and it needed little concentration once we had acquired the knack for it. One of us stood and assembled cardboard boxes, while the other two sat at the opposite side of the table to fill them with cubes; and we changed places every half hour, so that the work seemed less tedious and each had a chance to sit down. Each group was expected to pack a set amount of cubes each day, but the monotony of the work was lightened by our being able to chat as much as we liked. After the academic atmosphere of college, followed by my weeks at home, it was a refreshing change to spend a large part of my time chatting with other women. The machines here were much quieter, and did not make the deafening noise of the looms and winding-frames that had isolated me from my workmates in the mill, so we could talk and listen quite comfortably. But the best thing about this job, apart from the money, was knowing that my time there was limited. Unlike many of my workmates who would be forced to look for similar jobs once they finished here, I knew exactly where I was going and it was entirely my own choice. When the summer was over I would be off to Salford.

As I had expected, my part-time job had little effect on our domestic life. In the mornings, when Frank, Margaret, Sheila and Kevin had left for work and Maureen had gone to catch the school bus, I had time to wash the breakfast things and tidy the house before I went out myself, so that I would have only the evening meal to prepare when I came in. I had to walk along the main shopping street on the way home, so it was quite convenient for me to get the shopping then. With the automatic washing machine to take care of the laundry, and the children doing their own ironing, making their beds and cleaning their rooms, the remaining household tasks and the cooking were no trouble to me.

Maureen, our youngest child, was due to leave school at the end of the summer term, and was looking forward to starting a course at Accrington and Rossendale College. She wanted to work with people, caring for children or the elderly, and hoped the Home and Family Care course would equip her for this. It was strange to think that all our children were now grown up and independent. Officially, Maureen was still a child, but she seemed to have grown up a lot during her last year at school and I felt that the more adult atmosphere of college life would suit her. She thought so, too, and waited as eagerly as I had done thirty-six years earlier for July and the day she would leave school. But, before then, Frank had an accident at work.

It was a hot Friday towards the end of May, the start of the Spring Bank Holiday weekend. The workroom had been stuffy, I was having a heavy period and the walk home had seemed longer than usual. As I walked into the house, I was dreaming of a good cup of tea and a nice, relaxing bath. Frank was sitting there in his favourite armchair. It was only half-past three.

'Hello,' I said, surprised to see him home so early. 'Have you finished soon for Spring Bank?'

'No, I 'aven't, Win, I've 'ad an accident wi' t'mower. I were mowin' on a slope, an a bit o' wire got caught in t'blade. It caused t'machine to stop suddenly, an' it bounced back an' 'it me right in t'stomach. I've been to Casualty for X-rays an' I've to go back Sunday. Don't worry, though, I don't think it's owt serious, but it doesn't 'alf bloody 'urt!'

The X-rays showed that he had an umbilical hernia and would need surgery before he could go back to work. He had never been in hospital, and there followed several anxious weeks of boredom and pain while he waited for a vacancy in the men's surgical ward of Accrington Victoria Hospital. It came at last and, as I finished my twelve weeks' work at Oxo with enough money in the bank for our car deposit, Frank went into hospital for his first operation. He appeared to make a good recovery and, after a week, was allowed home with strict orders to rest and not to lift anything

heavier than a cup of tea. As the weeks went by, he grew restless
and impatient. Unable to tend the garden, he swore at the weeds
that grew among his carefully planted flowers and vegetables. The
boys tidied the flower-beds, lifted the rows of potatoes that were
ready, and dug over the soil where they had been; but they did
not have Frank's dedication and, in any case, he wanted to do
it himself. Forbidden to drive, he asked young Frank to collect
the small car he had chosen just before going into hospital. On
sunny days, he would sit in the front porch pretending to read,
and staring at the parked car over his opened book. By October,
he was allowed to drive on short journeys, and could manage small
tasks in the house, but gardening was still forbidden.

He had been assured that, if all went well, he should be back
at work within three months of the operation, but it was plain that
his return to full health was going to take longer than that. Always
strong and active, he had seldom lost a day's work through illness,
and he found this new situation worrying and difficult to accept.
As I left for my first day at university, despite his repeated
assurances that he would be all right, I was uneasy at the idea of
his being alone all day, to while away the time as best he could.

CHAPTER NINE

AN UNDERGRADUATE

I was to report to Colin Harrison at eleven, but before that there was the welcoming meeting for first-year students in Maxwell Hall. The Hall was crowded and, though most of the students were young college-leavers, there were quite a few older students, so I felt less noticeable than I had been that first day at Sandy Lane. After we had been addressed by the Vice-Chancellor and the Students' Union President, we all spilled out to report to our course tutors. Quite a large number disappeared inside Peel Building, where I had had my interview; and by the time I had climbed up to the fourth floor where Colin Harrison's room was, I was hot and breathless and at the wrong end of a long queue. For a few minutes I leaned against the wall to cool off and get my breath back, then I began to look round and wonder which of my companions would be taking the same subjects as me, and if any of them would become my friends. Then I noticed a familiar figure standing a few feet in front of me. I moved towards her quietly.

'Stella?'

My Accrington College friend turned round: 'Win! I heard you were coming here. Isn't it great? You're going to do English, aren't you? We can go to the lectures together.'

Stella's husband, Kevin, had died suddenly while she was on the A level course. She had bravely continued her studies, but had been undecided what to do when the course ended, for she and Kevin had been planning to take a degree course together. After his death, with twins Antoinette and Michael to consider, she had talked of going to Salford University, for their home was about halfway between Salford and Great Harwood and, like me, she could travel daily. And here she was.

'I thought it best to stay where we are in the circumstances. The twins've just started at St. Christopher's — they're eleven now. We have the house, and the area's familiar to them, so I might as well come here to take my degree.'

Although I had looked forward to going to university and meeting
new people, it was good to have Stella there and I knew she was
glad to have me, too. Together we went through the procedure
of becoming bona fide undergraduates, a far more complicated
business than I had ever imagined.

'Now don't you worry about a thing,' Colin Harrison told me,
as he examined my GCE certificates before passing them on to
his secretary for photo-copying. 'Any problems about the course
or whatever, you just come and see me. I'll lend you a shoulder
to cry on.'

'Thank you very much,' I said. 'But I hope I won't need it,
though I'll probably be glad of your advice before long.'

From Peel Building, we went to the Sports Hall to join the
hundreds of other students queuing for formal registration. We
signed forms, answered questions, collected leaflets on the
numerous societies run by students, and had our photographs taken
for our identity cards, before emerging in mid-afternoon for our
first cup of tea since leaving home.

'Ooh, Stella, I'm ready for this!' I exclaimed, as we sat down
in one of the many snack-bars scattered around the campus. 'D'you
know, if I were still at t'mill I'd've had five or six cups by this
time. This education lark's not as cushy as some folk like to make
out.'

As we sat there chatting, I was half-listening to other
conversations going on around us in so many different accents,
some foreign, some from different parts of Britain. At Accrington,
the dominant accent had been my own northern one, with slight
variations according to which local town or village the speaker
came from. Even the Asian students, sons and daughters of the
immigrants who had come to Lancashire in the early 'sixties to
work in the cotton mills, when not speaking Bengali or Punjabi
among themselves, had spoken English with a strong Lancashire
accent. Ironically, at northern Salford most of the regional accents
came from the South. Some of the speakers used what the BBC
used to call the 'Queen's English', and what I was soon to learn
was known in academic circles as 'Received Pronunciation'.

Snatches of conversation in voices heard on radio and television more than from real people made my new surroundings seem unreal, and made a stronger impression on me that first day than anything else. Yet, within two or three weeks, all those unfamiliar regional accents, and even the 'BBC' ones, had become commonplace to me, and I chatted with their owners as easily as I had with my workmates at Oxo earlier in the year.

There were no first-year lectures during the first few days at the University, and I spent most of my time there getting to know other students on the JASS course, sorting out my timetable, and attending meetings arranged by the different departments so that new students could meet their tutors. Stella was also on the JASS course and, for her first year, had chosen to study English, European Art, and History with Politics, so we would be attending several of the same lectures. Seminars and tutorials* would be arranged in consultation with the individual subject tutors, and we were invited to meet them at a sherry party on Friday afternoon.

'Imagine − me drinkin' sherry on a Friday afternoon when most folk are at work,' I said to Stella, as we strolled over to the AUEW** Building where the party was being held.

Stella winked. 'They're doing an Oxford, Win,' she laughed. 'You know, sherry parties, dreaming spires and all that. I can't see me having much time for dreaming, though, by the look of my timetable so far − it's horrific.'

'Yes, I know − mine's same. It's not History with Politics and Sociology with Psychology at all; it's History *and* Politics and Sociology *and* Psychology if me timetable's anything to go by. Leastways, there's separate lectures for each of 'em. We'd better make the most of this afternoon − it doesn't look as if we'll get much time to relax once we get started.'

---

* A lecture is a talk given by a lecturer while everyone else sits quiet and listens. A seminar is an exchange of ideas among a group of students, chaired by a tutor, on a particular topic. A tutorial is a talk prepared and delivered by one student to a small group of fellow-students and a tutor, who then makes 'frank' comments and asks awkward questions about it.

** AUEW stands for Amalgamated Union of Engineering Workers. Salford University is noted for its Industrial Centre.

At the sherry party, a pale young man in jeans and T-shirt came over and introduced himself as my Sociology tutor. He evidently knew who I was.

'How d'you think you'll cope, Mrs Bridges, with all these young students around all the time? I mean, you're bound to feel a bit out of place with so many of them so much younger than you, aren't you?' Mmm, I thought, we've got a right little bundle o' tact 'ere. 'E's probably already planning a study on 'The Conflicting Cultures of the Middle-Aged Working-Class Female Student and her Teenage, Middle-Class Counterpart', wi' me as 'is main research area.

But what I said was: 'Oh no, not at all. I've a houseful of teenagers at home, and I spent two years on a full-time A level course where most of the students were teenagers. There's a much wider age range here.'

Although I was generally accepted for what I was − one of the students − I was aware that the presence of a woman like me in a university was unusual. Had I not been, the reactions of some of the people I met would soon have made me aware of it. One of the English lecturers, a man of about my own age whose working-class parents had made sacrifices to give him a good education, was fond of talking as if he and I had come out of the Ark − the tradesmen's entrance, of course. Later on, he became my English tutor and I came to know more about him. He gave me the impression that as a young man he had found it difficult to fit in with his middle-class university companions and had blamed his parents, especially his mother − his coal-miner father being, as he contemptuously put it, 'merely a meal ticket' − for she had been 'in service' and, having seen how the other half lived and determined that her children would join them, had taken in washing to help pay for their education. Even now, though he was in middle age and looked the epitome of comfortably-off, middle-class respectability, the bitterness remained, only partly hidden by the cheerful benevolence with which he faced the world. Outwardly successful, he seemed to me rather a pathetic creature, incapable of fully enjoying his success, and I wondered if his ambitious mother might have done better to send him down the pit.

One morning, during the week following the sherry party, I stood in front of the JASS notice-board, pen and paper in hand, noting down the times and places of the tutorials I was to attend. I copied details of the History and Politics meetings, and noted that information for students of English was on another notice-board in the Modern Languages Department over in Crescent House. Then I came to the Sociology lists. To my dismay, I found that, unlike the other subjects for which there was one JASS tutorial each week, there were six marked down for Sociology. I checked the lists carefully, but there was no doubt about it. There were no fewer than six Sociology tutorials a week for the JASS course. I knew I would never manage to attend all of them. Brought up as I was to attend school and work regularly and punctually, a habit I had kept up all through the A level course, I couldn't abandon it lightly. I would have to see Colin Harrison and ask for his advice.

'Good heavens, Winifred!' he exclaimed, when I told him my problem. 'You surely don't think you're expected to attend *six* Sociology tutorials a week?'

'Well, that's the number on the notice-board,' I told him. 'I've checked.'

'Yes, but you just choose the one that's most convenient to you. Sociology happens to be very popular as a third subject on JASS, so we have to arrange a number of tutorials in order to accommodate the larger numbers of students taking it. One subject, one tutorial — and you won't find many students who'll attend even one *every* week.'

I thanked him sheepishly and left, feeling naive and foolish. But it had been a natural mistake given my background and, some time later, when I attended a lecture on the Sociology of Work and listened to the lecturer pontificating on the 'Protestant work ethic', I remembered the incident and smiled to myself at the irony of it. If only the lecturer had known, he had a perfect example of his subject sitting in front of him.

I had been right about the subjects being History *and* Politics, and Sociology *and* Psychology. Even English had four separate courses: Development of the English Language, Phonetics, Poetry, and Prose Fiction. As Stella had put it during that first week, the JASS timetable was 'horrific'. Dashing from lecture halls on the main campus to English lectures across the road in Crescent House, three or four times a day, did away with the need for 'PE', compulsory or otherwise; and until I grew used to it, I found the pace exhausting.

Travelling to and from the University took up a great deal of my time. Frank was not yet well enough to drive long distances, and I went by bus each day. My small-town upbringing had not prepared me for the heavy traffic of the city, and I dreaded crossing the busy roads on my way from the bus stop in Manchester to the University in Salford. I would stand on the edge of the pavement and wait for someone to come and stand beside me; then, as they crossed, I would scurry along behind them, fingers crossed, looking directly in front of me so as not to see the heavy lorries and fast cars that seemed to be bearing down on me from all directions. The return journey during the evening rush hour was even more daunting. For a short time, Stella helped me to avoid it by driving me to a bus stop in Prestwich two miles away, where I could catch the express from Manchester. It was a relief not to have to go into the city; but if we were a little late leaving the University and I missed the bus, I had over an hour to wait for the next one, and would arrive home at about eight o'clock, cold, tired, and in no mood for studying after my belated meal.

'You can't keep goin' on like this,' Frank remonstrated, when I walked in one evening soaked through after waiting for the bus in the pouring rain. 'You're goin' to end up wi' pneumonia standin' there in all that rain, an' then sittin' an hour on t'bus in them wet clothes. We'll 'ave to sort summat out.' And, being Frank, he did.

'I've cracked it, Win!' was his greeting when I came home the following evening. 'There's a train straight through from Blackburn every morning, an' it stops at Salford. There's trains runnin' back an' all, so I can drive you to t'station in t'morning' an' pick you up at night.'

That problem solved, I could get on with my university work and running the home. During my first term, while Frank was still unable to go back to work, he did the shopping and the lighter household tasks, while the rest of the housework was shared among the children living at home and myself, as it always had been. I still prepared the evening meal, partly for economic reasons and partly because cooking is the only bit of housework that I enjoy doing. Although I was at the University every weekday, there were two mornings each week when I did not have a 9.15 lecture and did not have to leave home until after eight. Wednesday was half-day at Salford, but I had a Psychology tutorial at twelve and did not get home until three. Every third Wednesday, I collected Catherine and Mandy, then aged nine and seven, from school for tea, after which we called for Laura and Heather, aged eight and three, to go to the library, visiting Candy Time, the nearby sweetshop, before delivering them all safely home around seven.

Our old-style family Sundays had come to an end soon after my Mum's death. Sheila and Kevin were both courting, Margaret had little Gemma to take care of, and Maureen divided her spare time between her boyfriend and her own college work. Mary seemed to have recovered from her depressive illness and was training for her nursing certificate, but she was still living-in at the hospital, so I still looked after Laura and Heather on Saturdays. Most of my Sunday was now spent studying. Margaret proved a great help, for she took on the cooking while I sat upstairs with my books.

The long lists of recommended reading given out by the University lecturers seemed incredible to me, compared with the limited number of set books on the O and A level courses. But after my experience with the Sociology tutorials, I did not need Colin Harrison to tell me that I was not expected to read them all. I soon realised that learning to choose the most relevant background reading was actually an important part of the course. Even so, studying what were, in effect, three separate courses at once was very demanding, and even many of the younger students confessed that they also found it hard going. I might well be working on a critical appreciation of Keats's 'Ode to a Nightingale' one minute, an assessment of a Jane Austen character for tutorial discussion the next; a History essay on the origins of the First World War in the morning, and a paper on the 'embourgeoisement of the working classes' for a Sociology tutorial in the afternoon.

'You know, Win,' Stella remarked one day, as we left Crescent House after an English lecture to dash across to Chapman for some History, 'I never seem to think any more since I came here − I mean *really* think, like I used to. There's no time for it on this course.'

'Well, now you come to mention it, most of my thinkin' 's done on the train. That's if I don't nod off as soon as I sit down − if I get a seat, that is. But I know what you mean; I used to be able to let me mind wander when I were walkin' round me windin' frame at Highams. Mind you, if you'd nothing to think about on a job like that, you might as well be a robot once you'd got used to t'mechanics of it.'

Later that day, as I waited for my train home on the bleak platform at Salford station, I thought of that conversation with Stella, and my mind went back to one evening when I was on the late shift at the mill. The time between returning to work at 6.15 after the half-hour break and finishing at ten seemed an eternity, so I had found a way of making it pass more quickly by dividing it up into segments. I would go to the loo at seven, brew-up at eight, make another visit at nine, then return to my frame at ten-past to busy myself filling up the hopper, changing the cones and making sure that all the broken ends were pieced up to give a good start to the young Pakistani who ran the machine on the night shift. On this particular evening, I climbed the narrow steps to the women's loos to find the normally bustling Lily leaning against the wall, staring in front of her as if in a dream.

'Hiya, Lily, penny for 'em,' I said, as she turned towards me. 'You were miles away then, weren't you.'

'Aye, I were, Winnie, I were just thinkin' to meself. I nipped up 'ere for a quick puff' − she waved her cigarette − 'an' I thought, blow it; work'll be 'ere long after I'm dead an' buried, I'm 'avin' a minute or two before I go back.' She paused, then: ' "What is this life, if full of care,/We have no time to stand and stare? . . ." '

And without a hint of self-consciousness she recited the complete poem beautifully, while I listened, secretly astonished by this unsuspected side of Lily's character. Now, six years later, standing on Salford station I visualised the rough-and-ready Lily reciting poetry during her brief escapes from the machine that dominated her life, and was thankful that I had taken the opportunity to escape for good. The course was hard, but I was doing what I wanted to do, not what I had to do. I no longer needed to spend my days day-dreaming and fantasising in order to make them bearable.

Running a home and living so far away from the campus meant that Stella and I missed out on a lot of the social activities enjoyed by most of the other students. But we did manage occasional visits to the Royal Exchange Theatre in Manchester for the Wednesday afternoon matinées, with a group of friendly young JASS students. They seemed unsure what to make of me at first, but quite soon accepted me as a friend with whom they could share jokes and grumbles, swap notes and essays and offer and accept help when needed. The common ground on which these university friendships were based was a world away from what I shared with my workmates at the mill and at Oxo; but the relationships between us were fundamentally the same, for in both cases we were all, more or less, in the same boat.

Inevitably, I found myself comparing the young people I met at Salford with my own children at home. Although these mainly middle-class youngsters were academically clever, they were surprisingly ignorant of many of the realities of life with which my working-class children were all too familiar. Some of them seemed to have formed their impressions of working-class life from watching *Coronation Street* or reading 'Andy Capp' cartoons in the *Daily Mirror*. Others, on the strength of having spent a few weeks of their summer holidays working in a factory or on a building site for spending money, would claim that such work was a 'doddle', or 'quite fun − once you get used to it'. This kind of remark was usually made when an industrial dispute was in the news and the speaker didn't see 'what on earth the so-called workers had to complain about'.

I once found myself − unwillingly, and uninvited − involved in an argument between members of the Young Conservative

Students' Society and supporters of their Socialist counterparts who happened to be sharing my table in the crowded snack-bar at Crescent House.

'Statistics prove,' declared one of the Conservatives, 'that more working-class people own their own homes, drive their own cars and have colour TVs, washing-machines, telephones and so on than was ever envisaged before the Second World War — or after it, for that matter.'

'Statistics!' spat out one of his opponents scornfully. 'They prove nothing. One day the workers of this country'll show the arrogant ruling classes that they've had enough of being exploited and down-trodden.' He warmed to his subject: 'There're millions of working people all over this country just waiting to overthrow the British political system, and show their exploiters just how the country ought to be governed.'

'Nonsense!' put in one of the others. 'As long as the men can afford to get drunk and the women can go to bingo, the working classes don't give a damn about politics.'

And so they went on, first one side and then the other, the arguments of each becoming more heated, and offering a more distorted view of working people, with every exchange. For a while I sat quietly, drinking my tea and trying to mind my own business, my eyes on the same page that I had been reading when the group had come to sit at my table. Then one of them came out with the remark: 'Working-class people are a lazy lot of ignorant morons. They know nothing because they haven't the brains to learn anything, and they're where they are because they're too bloody idle to make the effort to do anything else.'

I looked up from my book. The speaker was a belligerent-looking youth of about nineteen. 'If you don't mind me asking,' I said mildly, eyeing his smart clothes, expensive wrist-watch and the real leather briefcase he had placed carefully on the table in front of him. 'How many of these working-class morons do *you* know?'

'What?' he exclaimed, startled at my interruption and looking as surprised as if Marley's Ghost had suddenly appeared in front of him. Then, composing himself, he answered haughtily: 'I don't know any of them personally, I'm pleased to say. But I know all about them because . . .'

'Oh, you don't know any of them, but you know all about them, do you?' I broke in, sharply. 'Well then, you must be very clever in your own ignorant, moronic way.' I looked round at the others, now silent, waiting to hear what would come next. 'As a member of the class that you're all so knowledgeable about, I've heard more reasoned, well-informed argument in the factory yard than any of you will ever be capable of offering if today's performance is anything to go by.' Then I turned to the young statistician: 'Have you any statistics on how many working people, including middle-class workers, are having to claim Family Income Supplement because of their low pay? Or on how many families live in homes with inadequate heating and without indoor sanitation? And you,' addressing the revolutionary, 'what evidence have you to suggest that all these millions of workers can't wait for your grand revolution? Most working people just want to be left in peace to do their jobs and get on with their lives. Those who do take part in industrial action usually do it only as a last resort, in support of decent working conditions and fair wages and not from any tin-pot political motives.' I closed my book and picked up my things. 'God help us all if we've ever to depend on the likes of you to run the country.' Then, as a parting shot, 'One thing most working people have that you lot haven't is consideration for others − I've read one sentence at least a dozen times since you came in here.'

'What did they say to all that?' asked Frank that evening when I told him about it. The children were all out, Gemma was asleep upstairs, and we were sitting by the fire enjoying a quiet hour or two.

'I left before they 'ad t'chance to say owt to me,' I answered. 'They just sat there gawpin' at me.' I laughed. 'I can imagine what they said when I'd gone, though. "Interfering old busybody − who does she think she is, talking to us like that? Typical of the working classes when they get a bit of education." 'Course, it were nowt to do wi' me, but I felt that mad when I thought of our Margaret an' Sheila an' Kevin workin' away in t'factory while them lot were callin' workers morons, an' goin' on about

revolutions an' what 'ave you, when they know nowt about workin'
folk an' t'way we live. You know, Frank, I've found most students
to be right nice youngsters, interested in other people an' really
'elpful. But you get some of 'em, like that lot today, an' you wonder
'ow they ever got into a university, they're so ignorant. I'm sure
that, given t'chance, a lot o' workin'-class youngsters, an' that
includes ours, could run rings round some o' them.'

'Aye, well, Win,' said Frank, 'you should know by now, you
get them sort wherever you go.'

Early in 1980, our son Michael separated from his wife Jean, who
took Robert and Christopher to live with her new family. Unable
to stay in the council house that the family had shared at Waterfoot,
Michael came to stay with us for a few weeks, sharing Kevin's
room until he could get a place of his own, and travelling daily
to and from his job on regular nights at a Rossendale mill. At first,
Michael was heart-broken, especially by his separation from the
children. So that he could be near them and his work, he accepted
his sister Anne's offer to stay with her in Waterfoot for a while.

On the credit side, we also had two happy events about that time,
when Andy and Kathleen had a second son, Jon, and Carole and
David presented us with another granddaughter, Joanne. But in
February, Frank was notified by the Department of Health and
Social Security that he was 'required to attend' a medical tribunal
which would decide whether or not he was fit to return to work.
Our own doctor had refused to sign him off, knowing that he still
suffered considerable pain and discomfort in the region of his
injury, and that even the smallest physical effort left him tired and
irritable. The tribunal reported that the operation scar was 'well-
healed', and that, in their opinion, he was fit for work.

'They seemed to think I *wanted* to stop at 'ome,' he said, bitterly,
when he returned from the Health Centre where our doctor had
reluctantly given him his final certificate. 'One snipe-nosed bugger
even suggested me belly were swollen through drinkin' 'eavy.'
His face darkened. 'If I ever meet 'im outside . . .'

And so he returned to work, only to come home each evening
so exhausted that he could only wash, eat his meal and go to bed.

We both knew that he was not yet fit for manual work, but his request for an appeal against the tribunal's decision was turned down. His workmates were sympathetic and helpful, making sure that he did not lift anything heavy in the course of his work; but I knew how he hated to be dependent on them, and my heart ached for his hurt pride.

During late May and early June, we JASS students took our first-year exams. To go on to the second and third years of the course, I would have to pass in eight subjects: History, Politics, Sociology, Psychology, and four areas of English. Within two weeks, the results were posted on the official notice-boards: Stella and I had both passed everything, including the Anglo-Saxon, which gave me a special thrill considering my experience at Manchester University.

'Good lass, Win,' Frank congratulated me, grinning all over his face. 'I knew you could do it awright!'

'It were all them cups o' tea you made me when I were revisin',' I told him. 'I don't know what you put in 'em, but, by heck, it worked!'

Maureen also had good passes in her first-year college exams; Mary was doing well with her nursing studies; and there had been signs, during his last spell of leave from Germany, that she and John might get back together when he came home for good in a few months' time.

About halfway through the summer holidays I had a visit from a journalist, Geoff Rumney of the *Lancashire Evening Telegraph*. He told me that he had heard from a 'little bird' that I was taking a degree course, and asked if he could interview me for his occasional series featuring local personalities. He was pleasant and friendly, so I agreed to talk to him.

'Is it OK if I call you Winnie?' was his first question, then: 'Now, can I ask if you've got children and, if so, how many?'

After I had told him of our large family and he had recovered from the shock, he was fascinated to hear how we had coped when all the children were living at home. I explained how Frank and I, with my Mum's help, had managed to take care of the children

between us while he worked long hours and I did part-time work
when I could get it. 'Later, when the children were older and some
of them married, I was able to work full-time on shifts at Highams;
that's what I was doing when I first started going to evening
classes.'

'But what about when they were all at home? How on earth did
you do all the shopping and the cooking for thirteen of you?'

I told him how useful Frank's green fingers had been in providing
us with most of the vegetables we needed for the greater part of
the year. 'Then, during the winter, we used to have a half-
hundredweight of potatoes delivered weekly from a local shop,
along with all the basic groceries. I had a standing order for three
large loaves every day and six on Saturdays to see us through the
weekend, which one or other of us collected on the way home.
We had the milk delivered daily, of course, about fifty pints or
so each week at one stage, I remember.' I paused. 'As for the
cooking, I kept to the old Lancashire tradition of preparing food
that cooked itself while I was busy — real convenience food, I
call it.'

All this he noted down, together with some details of my early
life, how I had returned to education in middle age, and the degree
course I was taking; and a few days later, the article appeared
in the paper. It was an excellent write-up. As a result, everyone
in the town who knew me knew of my return to education and
my hopes of taking a degree. Whenever I went shopping, so many
friends and acquaintances stopped to congratulate me and to wish
me luck that the journey took me twice as long as it had before.
It was heart-warming to be on the receiving end of so much
goodwill and interest, and I believe that this friendly encouragement
from the people of my home town went a long way towards helping
me through the course.

After the first-year exams, I was able to drop Sociology and
Psychology. But I found this made little difference to the amount
of work I had to do, because the different aspects of History,
Politics and English that we studied in the second year became
more specialised and therefore more demanding. The essays and
tutorial papers we were now asked to write involved reading more

than just books. I found it exciting to discover snippets of information relevant to the topic I had chosen to write about after hours of scanning old newspapers and documents. This type of research was especially encouraged in the History Department, where our second-year studies were centred on British History since 1830. One of my tutorial assignments was to review a report in the *Manchester Guardian* of a Chartist meeting in Manchester in the late 1830s. I spent a long morning in Bolton Public Library, going through piles of dusty old newspapers to find the report, and returned home to write the paper feeling scruffy and thirsty from all that dust, yet oddly satisfied by the morning's work.

When I thought about it, I did not regret having chosen the Joint Honours course, despite originally wanting to take Single Honours in English. I was finding the History much more interesting than I had expected, and some of my first-year essays had prompted my History tutor to invite me to transfer to his Single Honours History course. But I felt that studying both subjects, though it was hard work, gave me the best of both worlds. Reading novels like Mrs Gaskell's *Mary Barton* and Dickens's *Hard Times* helped me to understand the social history of the nineteenth century, while the History lectures told me more about the times the writers had lived through: the two subjects were complementary. I also continued to enjoy the language content of the English course which, this year, consisted of Early Middle English and Traditional English Grammar, all of which kept me as fully occupied as I had been during the first year. By the end of term, though I had worked hard to keep up with all my course work, I still had essays to complete for History and Politics, exercises for my tutors in Grammar and English Language, and an English Literature essay, all to be handed in during the first week of the Spring term. So apart from a week of Christmas celebrations with the family, I spent all of my month's holiday working.

Just before the Easter break, all second-year JASS students reading History with Politics were given instructions for the presentation of the dissertation required as part of the degree. This was to be some eight to ten thousand words in length, on a topic chosen by the student, with the proviso that it must be political or historical in content. The student was required to research and write up the dissertation under the supervision of a member of staff selected with the approval of the Department's Chairman. A provisional title was to be handed in for approval during the first week of the Summer term, and the whole project completed and submitted by January the following year. January seemed comfortably distant. But putting together a dissertation was not as easy as it sounded.

CHAPTER TEN

LOVE, MARRIAGE AND A CRISIS

Meanwhile, our house was full of excitement because Margaret was to be married. During the previous summer, young Frank, a keen member of a local tug-o-war team, had taken her and Gemma, along with his three children, to several 'pulls', where she had met a member of the team, a burly young farmer named John. Frank and Kevin, also a team member, had helped the romance along, teasing poor Margaret unmercifully. On practice nights, they would march bow-leggedly into the house singing 'Oi've gotta brand new comboine 'arvester' in an exaggerated West-country accent. One night, they let us know that they had given John our phone number and Margaret could expect a call the very next evening. Sure enough, the call came, a date was made and kept, and now they were to be married. Margaret and Gemma, now a delightful, curly-haired three-year-old, would be leaving us to live in a village near the farm several miles away in the beautiful Ribble Valley. Mary was to be Matron-of-Honour and Gemma the bridesmaid. John's family had taken both Margaret and Gemma to their hearts, and we were all looking forward to the happy event.

But before the day came we had another family crisis. Maureen, now just past her eighteenth birthday, had got herself a part-time job at a Little Chef restaurant, to earn some spending money while she was at college. She had recently complained of bruises on her arms and legs, and at first we thought she must have bumped herself during busy spells at work. But one evening, about three weeks before the wedding, I noticed an ugly black bruise stretching from toes to ankle on her left foot.

'Have you dropped something on that foot, Maureen?' I asked.

'No. It's just gone like that.'

'Does it hurt?'

'No.'

121

I pushed the dreadful thought from my mind. 'You'd better see t'doctor,' was all I said.

The following Monday, summer term began. Stella and I were taking down details of the second-year exams, due to begin in less than three weeks, from the notice-board, but my thoughts were with Maureen and those ugly bruises.

'Oh Gawd!' drawled the girl next to us, who had never been known to turn up for the first lecture of the day at 9.15. 'Some of these grotty exams start at half-past nine! How the hell do they expect people to be properly awake at that time? It's the middle of the bloody night!'

Stella and I exchanged glances. She travelled from Edenfield every morning. It was nearer than Great Harwood to Salford, but it was far enough to travel, and she also had the twins to see to. I thought of my own children, who had left school at sixteen and had usually done half a morning's work by half-past nine. No wonder some folk regarded students as pampered and over-privileged if they only ever came across her type, I thought.

Maureen had an appointment with the family doctor on the Tuesday.

'I haven't to go to college tomorrow,' she reported. 'I've to go to the Health Centre for a blood test.'

I arrived home on Wednesday afternoon to find her waiting for me.

'I've to ring up for me result next Tuesday. It can't be anything serious, Mum, or I'm sure I wouldn't have to wait *so* long.'

That evening, while I was scanning the shelves in the local library for some guidance on Joyce and D. H. Lawrence, I felt a gentle tap on my shoulder, and turned to see Kevin standing there.

'Mum, you'll 'ave to come home — t'doctor's at our house an' our Maureen's to go into hospital right away — he's ringin' for an ambulance now.'

The word 'leukaemia' seemed literally to appear before my eyes. It pressed on my brain and echoed through my mind.

At the hospital, I sat in the corridor outside the ward while Maureen was put to bed and examined. It was nearly visiting time and, as the minutes ticked by, I was dimly aware that the queue of visitors was growing. People were becoming restless as time passed. Someone muttered, 'What the hell's goin' on in there?'

'Bedpans, probably,' came another voice.

'They should sort that out before now − it's goin' to be time to go 'ome before we get to go in!'

At last they were allowed in, and I was left alone with my thoughts. Sitting beside me in the ambulance, Maureen had made me promise to go to Salford as usual the following day: 'You'll only sit there worryin' if you don't go, Mum, an' I'm sure there's no need. I feel OK, an' I think I look OK, don't I?' In her trendy shirt and high-heeled, knee-length boots, jeans fashionably tucked in, carefully made-up eyes shining, she certainly looked healthy enough.

After a while, I was allowed into the ward to sit by her bed. She kept up her carefree front, but I knew that underneath she was just as scared as I was. The ward sister tried to reassure me: 'We're going to do some tests, Mrs Bridges. Maureen's general health seems good, and she's in good spirits. It's always a little frightening when a patient is brought in without warning. I really can't tell you anything until the tests are done and the results come out. You can ring us whenever you like. And do try not to worry.'

I made all the right noises and left without uttering the dreaded word, as if I could keep the disease itself at bay if I refused to name it aloud. But I knew very well that Sister was telling me 'nowt', only keeping me from asking awkward questions. That was part of her job.

The following evening, Maureen was pale and subdued, though she tried to be cheerful. She had had a painful bone marrow test and several blood tests. Sister was off duty and the staff nurse could tell us nothing, she said: 'When the results of the tests come through, Dr Ward will explain everything.' And I had to be content with that.

Next morning, the ward sister telephoned me: 'Could you come in and see Dr Ward at eleven o'clock, Mrs Bridges?' Young Frank drove me to the hospital. Dr Ward, a fatherly-looking man, was waiting with Sister in her office.

'Your daughter is quite ill, Mrs Bridges. But she hasn't got leukaemia, as I'm sure you feared.'

I was so relieved that I only half-listened while he explained what was wrong with Maureen, and prescribed a course of tablets which he hoped would solve the problem. 'If they don't do the trick,' he warned, 'it might be necessary to remove her spleen.' This sounded dreadful, but not nearly as dreadful as leukaemia.

'Off you go and see Maureen now,' beamed Sister, 'and *smile!*'

She had no need to tell me. As we walked along the corridor towards the ward, I told young Frank the good news and the bad news.

'Her spleen!' he exclaimed, looking shocked. 'You don't look all that worried, Mum.'

'No. And you'd better not look worried, either. Get smiling,' I told him. 'Sister's orders!'

Later, Maureen confided that she had known what the bone marrow test was for, but she had said nothing, so as not to worry me: 'You see, we'd been learning about blood diseases in Biology at college just a week or two before I were ill,' she said. 'God, I were scared to death when they fetched all that paraphernalia, an' told me what they were doin', but I didn't let on I knew what it were for, 'cause they might've told you.'

But now, as her brother and I approached her bed, grinning like two Cheshire Cats, all she asked, as Sheila had done six years earlier, was, 'What about the wedding? Will I be home in time?'

Luckier than Sheila, she *was* home in time, and what a wedding it was! Margaret looked lovely in her Empire line dress; with her thick glossy hair hanging in ringlets under a lacy picture hat, she might have stepped out of a Gainsborough painting. Outside the church, a crowd of workmates waited to carry her shoulder-high around the churchyard, with her lucky blue garter exposed for all to see. John summed up the happiness of the day at the reception when he raised his glass and said, 'Eeh, it's been a grand day — t'best day o' me life!'

I looked round at the smiling guests, at John's family, at Gemma and her cousins looking unusually angelic in their wedding finery, at my own children, happy in Margaret's happiness. I caught Frank's eye, and we both glanced at Maureen chatting gaily to her boyfriend Stephen as if her illness had never been.

Late that evening, when Margaret and John had left for a short honeymoon and all the excitement was over, we talked quietly of the day's events.

'Aren't we lucky!' said Frank, as so often before. 'All these children, an' we've managed to see 'em all grow up strong an' 'ealthy.'

'Ah, well,' I replied, 'you know what me Mum allus said — ''God's good an' t'Devil's not so bad if you keep thick to 'im.'' '

And on that happy note we slept.

CHAPTER ELEVEN

COUSIN MAY

The Monday following Margaret's wedding was the day we began the second-year exams. After the weeks of anxiety over Maureen, the relief of her recovery, then the pleasure and happiness of the wedding, the exams hardly seemed to matter; and perhaps because of this, I felt relaxed and found them less difficult than I expected.

'It didn't seem to matter all that much whether I passed or not,' I told Stella afterwards when we were discussing the papers. 'I've been so strung up these last few weeks that I don't seem to care what happens so long as Maureen's all right. Anyway, they're over with now, and there's nothing I can do but wait for the results.'

When the results came out, I *had* passed; but what pleased me far more was to hear that Maureen, despite her weeks off sick from college, had achieved a first-class pass in her final exams.

I planned to spend the summer break, or as much of it as I could, collecting material for my final-year dissertation. Its title was to be *Social Policy and the Working Classes in the Late Nineteenth and Early Twentieth Centuries,* and I hoped to find some information on the half-time system in Lancashire and the reasons for the cotton workers' strong opposition to its abolition. During the early part of the vacation, I visited local history libraries in Great Harwood and Blackburn, and the Public Records Office in Preston, to examine old newspaper reports, union records and other documents for evidence to support my theory that the system existed for as long as it did because of the reluctance of the cotton workers to accept State help — to forfeit their hard-won independence and, with it, their respectability. In the years before the First World War, the wages of half-timers, small as they were, formed an important part of the family budget. Just as the attitudes of my parents' generation towards their children had been affected by the experiences of having lived through the depression of the 1930s, so (I believed) the attitudes of their parents and grandparents had

126

been influenced by the effects of the Cotton Famine of the late 1860s, when many cotton workers and their children had died of starvation, and those who survived had been forced to enter the workhouse as paupers. By the beginning of the First World War, the industry had recovered, and the demand for cotton goods had made many Lancashire families comfortably off compared with working people in many other parts of the country. But memories of hardship remained and, with them, fears that the relative prosperity the workers enjoyed might be only too short-lived. The wages of cotton workers were not high, but the earnings of children could boost the family income to a level well above the average income of those in other industries where the father was the only breadwinner. Besides, ever since the days of the handloom weavers, child labour had been a feature of the textile industry. The parents of many half-timers might have entered the mills at the age of nine or ten, working longer hours than their own children; and so, to them, there was nothing wrong in sending twelve-year-olds to work in the mills. I believed that this reasoning, together with the desire to remain independent of the State and, therefore, respectable in the eyes of their peers, was the key to the reluctance of the cotton workers to see an end to the half-time system.

By September, I had gathered quite a lot of evidence on the general theme of my project, but little on the subject of the half-time system apart from voting statistics on its abolition. I asked one or two former half-timers I knew if they would talk to me about their experiences, but they preferred not to, so I began to write the outline of the project anyway, hoping that the material I had managed to collect would be enough to satisfy my supervisor that my argument was feasible.

Then, one afternoon, I had a stroke of luck in the form of a telephone call.

'Is that Winnie?' asked the female voice on the other end of the line. 'We haven't met, but I found your number in the book. My name's May Beatty, and your father, Jim, was my cousin.' She explained that, while reading a magazine, she had been delighted to find, printed as a poem, the words of a song my Dad

had often sung as a small boy at family gatherings. 'Would you
like a copy of the words?' she asked. 'I could post it to you or,
if you like, you could come and collect it — I'd love to meet Jim's
girl.'

The following afternoon, I visited May in her tiny council flat,
about fifteen minutes' walk from our house. She greeted me
warmly: 'It's lovely to see you. Jim used to call on me quite often,
and he told me about you and your lovely family. I was very fond
of him — he was always so gentle, even as a boy. I can see him
now,' her eyes taking on a dreamy look, 'standing there, shoulders
back, hands clasped behind him, singing that very song I told you
about. He couldn't have been more than eight or nine years old
— he'd a beautiful voice and knew how to put his heart into a
song.' She sighed. 'They were such happy days in spite of us all
being so poor.'

Over a cup of tea, I told her of my own memories of Dad's
singing: 'He was very proud that, as a boy soprano, he'd once
sung with Dame Clara Butt, the famous contralto. I don't remember
what the occasion was, but he often spoke of it. He never lost
his love of music and singing — and neither did my Mum. I expect
you know they met when they were both members of St. Hubert's
choir.'

May nodded, smiling. 'She was a grand little woman was
Frances.'

I agreed. 'You know, one of my earliest memories of my Mum
and Dad is of hearing them singing together as I lay in bed with
our Betty. Mum always used to tell us she were a contralto. I don't
know about that, but I used to think it were lovely lying there
listening to 'em. Their voices blended perfectly to me as they sang
all their favourites from *Maytime, Bitter-Sweet,* and *Girl of the
Golden West.* You know, May, all those old Nelson Eddy/Jeanette
MacDonald favourites.'

'Oh yes, I remember all those,' May replied, 'and I remember
Cousin Jim singing in the shows they used to put on in St. Hubert's
School hall. He was in *The Pirates of Penzance* once, and I went
to see it with my sister Claire.'

'I can just remember being taken to see him in *The Gondoliers.*

I thought I were everybody 'cause my Dad were singing in front of all them people – it's been a favourite of mine ever since.'

'Oh it *is* nice to talk about old times like this!' May exclaimed, pouring me another cup of tea. 'Poor Jim, he didn't have an easy life, being the eldest of a large family and his father an invalid. Auntie Lizzie, your Grandma Lord, used to say she'd never have managed without Jim's help. I often thought he'd have made something of himself if he hadn't had to go to work at such an early age.' She sighed again. 'But then, we all had to in those days.' And she began to tell me of how she herself had hoped to become a teacher, but had had to leave school to work in t'mill to boost the family income. 'I loved school and I loved learning, but it made no difference. When I was about ten, something like that, the teacher said to me one day, "May, how would you like to sit for a scholarship and go to the Convent School, and perhaps train to be a teacher?" I ran all the way home to ask my mother; I could picture myself in Convent green. But no. It wasn't to be – my future was already established for me. I was to become a half-timer at twelve, and leave school for good at thirteen, to work full-time in the mill.'

May's story was just what I had been looking for to reinforce the documentary evidence I had collected for my dissertation. When I told her this, unlike me she was delighted to be 'a bit of history'.

'If I come again and bring my tape recorder, will you tell me again about your days as a half-timer? Just tell me in your own words as you did this afternoon. I can't tell you how helpful it would be.' And so we arranged a second meeting. Soon I had my recording and had made a new friend. My Dad had often spoken of his cousin May, who had finally managed to leave the mill as a young woman and had gone to live and work in Manchester, quite a daring thing for a young working-class woman to do in those days. Although she had been back in Great Harwood for years, and my Dad had visited her occasionally, I had never met her until now. Her story was fascinating. She had been the eldest of five children of a weaver and his wife, who worked as a cleaner to earn some extra money for the family. 'When I was about seven or eight years old,' May recalled, 'about six in the morning Mother would wake me up. "Come on, May," she would say, "we've got to get up yonder." "Up yonder" being some new houses that were being built at the other end of town for the better class of people. The houses had boarded floors, and kitchens tiled from floor to ceiling, and we had to scrape all the plaster from the walls and then get down on our hands and knees to scrub the floors.' Her face grew serious as she thought of her stolen childhood. 'I used to help Mother with this arduous work until eight o'clock, when I would go home and wake the little ones, give them breakfast, get them ready and take them to school.' Then, as if in defence of her parents, especially her mother: 'But we weren't unhappy. Mother was always there waiting for us with a good meal ready when we came home for dinner; she did all her own baking. I can see it now — hot muffins on top of the oven. We used to have the muffins for tea with butter and golden syrup.' She smiled at the memory, then went on to repeat her story of how she had become a half-timer.

'I hated the mill, but I had to accept it, there was nothing else for it in those days. My sister Margaret was less dutiful than I was — she went to the mill, too, but she spent most of her time strolling round the weaving shed acting the lady. I was earning about ten shillings a week on my own two looms by this time — but not Margaret, oh no.' She shook her head. 'She earned very little in the way of money. She managed to earn herself a fitting nickname, though — "Miss Wag-arse" the men used to call her. Anyway, her antics got her out of the mill and into a gown shop — not the sort of occupation working-class girls were expected to take up in those days. I must admit I wasn't very pleased, and you should've heard the neighbours when they found out about it. "Thinks itsel' summat better than us," they said, "an' owt to be put in it place." '

Later, Margaret had gone to work as a nanny for a Blackburn businessman. 'She used to come home once a week on her day off,' May remembered. 'Ooh, Winnie, she did used to annoy me! I used to go with her to see her safely on the bus back, and she'd stand on the platform — the bus entrance was at the back in those days — and she'd wave at me and call out: "Bye-bye, May deah,

Ai'll give you a ring.'' And me working in the mill all day with
no idea how to use a telephone!'

CHAPTER TWELVE

MRS SEED

The piece of good luck over May was soon followed by another. Waiting my turn in the butcher's one day, I was approached by an acquaintance who had heard I was looking for former half-timers to interview. 'My mother would be happy to talk to you,' she said. 'Just give me a ring when it's convenient, and I'll arrange it with her.'

Mrs Seed was nine years older than May, but her memory of her girlhood was every bit as clear. Not a native of Great Harwood, she came from the little village of Mitton, some five miles away in the heart of the countryside.

'We moved to Harwood when I was nine years old,' she explained.

'It must have seemed very strange to you,' I remarked, 'coming to live in a noisy mill town, overshadowed by all those smoking chimneys, after being brought up in the country.'

'Well, it did at first, but I soon got used to it — I had to.'

Like May, Sarah Seed had entered the mill as a half-timer at the age of twelve. At first, she had accepted her fate meekly, although, as she told me, 'The walk from the weaving shed to the warehouse was a terrible journey to me, but I had to do it as it was part of my job to carry the cuts* from the looms to be inspected in the warehouse. The alleys between the rows of looms were so narrow that I had to walk sideways to avoid being hit by the picking-sticks which drove the shuttles across the looms . . . When I was seventeen, I asked my mother if I could leave the mill and train to be a nurse so that I could go to China as a missionary,' she went on, 'but I had to stay in the mill — my mother said I might get into trouble if I went away from home.'

---

* A cut is the length of cloth taken from the loom when the mark signifying that the correct number of yards has been woven shows on the cloth.

Later, Sarah married a young man who became well known in
Great Harwood as secretary of the local branch of the Weavers'
Union. Both were unemployed during the depression of the
'thirties, and, when conditions in the cotton trade began to improve,
they had great difficulty finding jobs in the town's mills because
of their close association with the Union. This had caused them
a lot of hardship, but the later cotton boom and acceptance of the
Union by employers brought them better times.

'Then,' she said, smiling, 'I was able to swap me clogs for shoes
to wear to work.'

After telling me her story, this amazing lady took me outside
to admire her well-kept garden, which she tended herself. During
the year before my visit, at the age of eighty-eight, she had fulfilled
a lifelong wish to visit the Holy Land. Now ninety-six, Mrs Seed
still lives alone and, although she is no longer able to do her own
shopping, and relies on her daughter to take her out, she still does
her own housework and cooking. She taught a weekly ladies' class
at her church and could be seen, rain, snow or shine, walking to
the meeting when she was well past her ninetieth birthday, before
failing eyesight prevented her from going out alone. The hardiness
of Mrs Seed's generation of working-class people brings to mind
students like the one who thought half-past nine was 'the middle
of the bloody night', and I wondered what she would make of
Sarah's story – and what Sarah would think of her.

I returned to the University in October, relieved that my History
project was well on its way. During the summer, I had made two
new friends; and in July, Frank and I had gained another grandson
when Stuart was born to Eileen and Billy.

It was my final year at Salford. By now, our bedroom was filled
almost to bursting point with the paraphernalia of my studies. In
one corner was a tall, narrow bookcase we had picked up from
a sale one bank holiday: it was tucked tightly between the wall
and a small chest of drawers, to keep it from toppling over with
the weight of the books I crammed on to its shelves. In the opposite
corner was our double bed and, at its foot, standing against the
wall, the wardrobe. The large, old-fashioned dressing table had

long since been exiled, and now stood in Margaret's old room.
In its place was my small second-hand desk-bureau, at which I
worked. Beneath the window, at a sideways angle to the bed, was
a solid, wooden bedding-box that had once belonged to Frank's
parents. All the stuff that would not fit anywhere else tended to
find its way on to the lid; while in the space underneath the bedding-
box I kept the portable typewriter Frank had bought me during
my time on the TOPs course. What with books, folders, handouts, newspapers, magazines and tapes, there wasn't room to swing
a cat, so it's a good job Frank is a patient man. He put up with
all this for years, with nothing more ill-tempered than an occasional
long-drawn-out sigh and his famous 'tut'. He encouraged me all
the way. That Christmas, even his present to me was chosen
specially to help with my final-year study of seventeenth century
literature: a small but well-produced copy of the King James
Authorised Version of the Bible.

Come November, I was worrying more and more about Frank:
he had had to have numerous tests and examinations as well as
several X-rays, but no apparent cause could be found for his
continuing pain. The doctor put him on the out-patients' list for
further investigation by the surgeon who had performed the
operation and, after weeks of waiting, he was given an
appointment. Within a few days of seeing the surgeon, he was
readmitted to hospital for more surgery. It turned out that after
the original operation, he had developed an infection: the internal
stitches had failed to dissolve and abcesses had formed in the wall
of his abdomen. For nearly two years, Frank had been working
with the infection building up inside his body. No wonder he had
been so tired all the time.

Just a week before Frank was due to go into hospital, young
Frank's wife Barbara left him without warning, taking the children
with her to Scotland, to stay with her mother. I had known that
the marriage was going through a difficult spell, but had not
expected this, and I missed the children almost as much as my
son did, as they had lived so near by and always been close and
loving. There was nothing I could do about them, but I could help
Frank. I visited him in Accrington Victoria Hospital every night,

coming home at about half past eight to spend the long evenings alone, working on the final draft of my dissertation. I hoped to have it ready for typing up during the Christmas break, and off my hands well before the deadline at the end of January.

Christmas 1981 was a quiet one for us, without the company of young Frank, Barbara and their three children. Sheila, Kevin and Maureen each had busy social lives of their own, and Frank, convalescing once more, was not up to much seasonal merriment. We spent those evenings quietly, just the two of us, and by the time the new term started he was up and about, and seemed to be making good progress.

'Well, Win,' he said, happily, 'it's 1982, t'year you'll get your degree − an' am I goin' to get drunk that day!'

CHAPTER THIRTEEN

FINAL DEMANDS

'Comin' to university every day's interferin' wi' me studies,' I remarked one morning to my small group of JASS students at a seminar on Joyce's *Ulysses*. 'I'm spendin' all me time at lectures an' seminars an' tutorials, an' it's leavin' me no time to get on with any work.'

They laughed. 'Yes, well coming to university does rather get in the way when all you want is to get a degree. But I know what you mean, Win. They told me when I'd done my A levels that the worst was over. An arts degree was supposed to be a doddle, by all accounts.'

'I was told the same,' one of the boys agreed. He sighed. 'I had visions of living it up half my time here and sleeping it off the other half, but no such luck. I get no chance to live it up, and I can't even sleep without dreaming of old Lear out on the heath in the storm. I could stand that, but last night the silly old fool was living it up himself with the Duchess of Malfi, while I stood on guard outside the cave!'

As the final exams loomed, there seemed to be more and more work. Several of my younger friends had stopped going home for weeks at a time. They spent their weekends trying frantically to finish essays, or waiting anxiously for their last one to be returned. More than once, I found myself offering a motherly and sympathetic ear to a worried young student. Not that I found the work any easier to cope with than they did, but one of the advantages of being a mum as well as a student was that I could take a more philosophical view of the whole thing. Of course, I wanted a good degree in return for all the hard work I had put into the course. And I wanted it for Frank as much as for myself, after all the encouragement he had given me. I had expected to spend all my working life in a mill or a factory, but here I was on a university degree course, making the most of myself, not only academically, but as a person. On the way from evening classes to university, I had gained the self-confidence that so many working-class people of my generation simply do not have, and had become aware of my own value as an individual whose ideas and opinions were as valid as anyone else's. There were still times, as I sat in seminars, tutorials or the coffee bar discussing politics, literature or history, when I mentally pinched myself to ascertain that it really was me, Winnie Bridges, coming out with all this academic argument. But it *was* me and I *had* made it to university. Degree or no degree, nothing could alter that. But I was a mum first.

In February, Sheila, by then an attractive twenty-one-year-old, announced that she and her boyfriend were moving into a flat in Accrington, near the greetings card factory where she had worked since leaving the slipperworks two years earlier. We were not old-fashioned, but it was not easy for Frank and me to let our daughter go with our blessing. Frank more than me was unhappy at the idea of Sheila and Steve 'livin' o'er t'brush', but I saw no point in quarrelling about it, especially as so many young couples had started living together before they married.

'She's twenty-one now, Frank,' I reminded him. 'At least she's been honest with us and told us what she's doin'. Anyway, she's made 'er mind up, an' if we try to talk 'er out of it she'll only be more determined. This way, we can all stay friends, an' then if she wants to come 'ome it won't be as 'ard for 'er to say so. Besides,' I added, 'at least we'll get a night's sleep when 'e's not ringin' up at all hours, an' she's not stood in t'lobby 'alf o' t'night, talkin' to 'im on t'phone.'

So Sheila moved out, and Frank took her and her suitcases to the flat. As they drove away, I thought back to my early days with Frank. After we married, we had moved in with my Mum and Dad until we could get a place of our own. Nowadays, I thought, they move into a place of their own, then get married if they feel like it.

Sheila had no sooner gone when Mary telephoned: 'Mum, could you do me a favour? I can't stop 'ere any longer. D'you think me an' t'girls can use our Sheila's room 'til we can get a flat or something? It won't be for long, an' we won't be any trouble. I'll tell you what it's all about when I see you.'

'My God!' I thought, 'there's more problems in this family than Marje Proops deals with in a month o' Sundays.'

'I'll ask your Dad,' I said, and went back upstairs to struggle with an essay on, of all things, Milton's *Paradise Lost*. As I turned the pages of my book to find the reference I needed, I caught sight of the words: ' . . . our Grand Parents in that happy State,/Favour'd of Heav'n so highly, . . .' 'You can say that again, John,' I said to myself. 'You must've 'ad me an' Frank in mind when you were writin' that.'

Next day, Mary came home to Mother. I arrived home to find them settling in. The girls would share Sheila's room, and Mary would go in with Maureen. As I walked in, five-year-old Heather came bouncing downstairs. She hugged me and grabbed my hand, pulling me along: 'Come an' look at our room, Gran, we've made it right nice. Ooh, aren't you glad you've got a houseful o' kids again?'

I would not have described Laura and Heather as a 'houseful o' kids', but I knew that having young children in the house again was bound to make a difference to my routine. But all being well, Mary and John would soon be back together. Apart from the time that John had spent in Germany and Mary had lived at Brockhall, they had lived for most of their married life with John's mother.

'It can't have been all that easy for 'er,' I said to Frank. 'After all, we were glad enough to get away from me Mum and Dad's 'ouse when we were young, an' I'll bet they were thankful to 'ave t'place to themselves after nearly three years o' sharin' it wi' us.'

'Aye,' Frank agreed, ''appen they'll get a place o' their own an' get together again before long.'

The new arrangement worked quite well. Mary was now a qualified nurse and worked long hours at the hospital, leaving home at six in the morning and returning at nine in the evening. If I had no early lecture to attend on the days she was working, I had just enough time to get the children's breakfast and see them off to school before leaving to catch my train. On her days off, Mary saw to the children herself, and cooked the evening meal before I came home.

Unable to work, Frank had become restless and depressed. No longer making good progress, he was in a kind of limbo between feeling well enough to want to do things and not being physically able to do them. So the children were a blessing in disguise: on the days when Mary and I were both away, Frank saw them to school and was glad of their company when they came home. The splits between Mary and John, and young Frank and Barbara, had affected him more deeply than he cared to admit. It had become clear that our son's marriage was over. Young Frank had a new partner, Janet, and Barbara had filed for divorce. He was fighting for access to the children, but without much success. Scotland was too far away for him to visit them regularly, and he missed them desperately. If he could gain 'staying access', the children would be able to spend holidays at his home, and stay in touch with the rest of the family. There was no doubt that he was happy with Janet and her two-year-old daughter, Leanne, but he spoke of his own children with sadness in his eyes.

'I don't know,' Frank ruminated, 'I can't understand these young 'uns today. They go mad to get wed, an' next time you look they've 'ad a row an' separated. I can't reckon 'em up.'

'Well, I used to wonder where we'd gone wrong,' I said, 'but I think it's just that times've changed – though I do still sometimes wonder if you an' me've made married life look too easy 'cause we allus seem to 'ave got on together so well. I mean our children might 'ave got th'impression that it were as easy as it looked, an' not realised that it takes so much effort to make a marriage work.'

'Aye, 'appen I should 'ave put me foot down wi' a firm 'and an' shown you 'oo were t' boss a bit more often.'

'Oh, aye,' I retorted, 'an' a fat lot o' good it would 'ave done you an' all!'

Government cutbacks in university funding had hit Salford particularly hard. When Prime Mnister Thatcher paid a visit, she was greeted by an impressive demonstration. Rows of black-clad students lined her route to the Industrial Centre, while a black-draped coffin representing the death of university education was carried by other students also dressed in black. The complete silence throughout the demonstration gave a dramatic effect to the whole scene, though it had little practical effect, for the cuts went ahead as planned.

During our few free periods, we students would discuss our future prospects. At least, the others would, for, true to my usual form, beyond a vague hope that I might find a place in adult education, I had no definite plans. Since I had started at university, unemployment had steadily increased, making it difficult even for graduates to find jobs. One or two of my friends spoke of taking post-graduate courses if their degrees were good enough, but I had no such thoughts. I knew that I would need to find something to occupy my mind when the course ended, but first I planned to have a break from studying and take life easy for a bit.

During the Easter vacation, Michael was married for the second time. His bride, Kathryn, looked beautiful in white, and after the ceremony at St. Alban's Church in Blackburn, we went on to a reception buffet at a nearby pub. Kathryn's sister and two of our daughters, Anne and Margaret, were noticeably pregnant: as they glided along to the dance music, one of the boys quipped, 'I thought all t'ships 'ad been requisitioned by Maggie, an' sent to t'South Atlantic.'

'Watch it, you,' warned Margaret, 'or I'll come over there an' sit on your knee!'

Everyone laughed, but we didn't find it funny when only weeks later the Falklands 'question' suddenly became the Falklands War, with the tragic loss of so many young lives.

When we returned to Salford after the Easter break, we crowded round the JASS notice-board for the last time, to find that all four English exams for the final degree were to be held during the same week. They were all timetabled for the mornings, between 9.15 and 12.15. As I noted down the times, I realised that the History exam had been arranged for the Tuesday afternoon, the same day as Modern Studies in English, so that those of us taking English and History for the JASS degree would be sitting two three-hour exams in one day.

'It's going to be hard going for you, Win,' sympathised Stella, when I pointed out this timing. 'You're going to have to leave home early every morning, and on the Tuesday you won't get home until pretty late.'

'No,' I replied. 'It'll be a twelve-hour day, at least. I've got used to those since I came here, an' t'family's got used to 'em, too. But two exams in one day seems a bit much. In fact,' I added, 'four English exams in one week doesn't seem all that fair. Never mind, at least we'll get 'em all over with quickly.'

The first exam of each year was the one that I always felt most nervous about. I felt that if I got through that one reasonably well, I could relax when I came to the rest. For the final year, our first paper was English Grammar and Lexicography.* I had a habit of jotting down a few notes the night before an exam, and reading them on the train to Salford.

'I might forget 'em all as soon as I sit down,' I said to Frank as I made sure the notes were in my bag before leaving home, 'but they put me in t'right frame o' mind, an' make me feel more confident, an' that's 'alf o' t'battle when you're takin' an exam.'

As I entered the large room in Maxwell Hall to take the exam, countless fingers were being metaphorically crossed for me back in Great Harwood. It seemed that the whole town was wishing me well: all the family; my former workmates; my O level friends; the lollipop lady who had always taken an interest in my 'academic career'; and May, in the confectioner's shop, only recently widowed, who had spared me enough thought in her grief to light a candle in church as an offering to God for my success. I hoped I would not disappoint them.

Now I sat down at the table with my number on it. We all had a number on the set of printed rules we were sent, along with details of Degree Day and information on the hiring of caps and gowns for the occasion. The gown hire firm had introduced a note of cheer into their information leaflets by giving details on how to reclaim the advance hire fees in the event of failure.

---

* Lexicography at Salford consisted of a series of lectures, seminars and tutorials on the history of dictionaries and their compilers. A favourite of mine is Eric Partridge's *Dictionary of Slang*.

At the given signal, I opened the question book and began to read. I was relieved to find a question that I thought I could answer. Once I had begun writing, I became absorbed in the paper and wrote almost non-stop for the whole of the three hours, which seemed to fly.

'I'll be OK now,' I told Frank when he asked how the paper had been. 'It's always same − once I've got t'first 'un over I can cope wi' t'rest, so I'll be OK.'

But I was not as OK as I thought I would be. At fifty-two, I was still a healthy woman. While at Salford, I had only ever had an odd day off sick. I still occasionally had heavy periods, but in recent months there had been nothing, and I presumed that I was going through the menopause. I felt well and thought myself lucky not to have 'hot flushes' and the like. Besides, my studies had kept me too busy to notice any such symptoms. In short, I believed it was a case of mind over menopause.

On the Tuesday morning, I set off to catch my train with jottings on Modern Studies in English and West European History safely in my bag. I planned to read the English notes on the train, as usual, and there would be time to read the History ones during the lunch break before the afternoon exam. Once again, my little trick seemed to work, and I got off to a good start with the Modern Studies paper. I was so involved in the question on the Transmission of Shakespeare's Texts that I left myself with hardly enough time to answer the questions on Leavis and Eliot and their views on the place of English Literature in the culture of our modern society. All the same, as I handed in the paper, I felt fairly optimistic about my chances of passing. When my English tutor came over and spoke to me I stood up, grateful for a chance to stretch my legs. Something trickled wetly down them. Horrified, I glanced down to see a small pool of blood spreading round my feet. Somehow, I managed to answer the tutor's question and he turned away to speak to someone else. I caught Stella's eye and pointed silently at my feet. Without a word, she took my arm, guided me to the back of the room to collect my bag and led me to the nearest washroom. As I washed, she organised an emergency service, sending two of the girls to the Union shop for fresh tights and underwear, leaving another girl to keep an eye on me, and herself going to the Medical Centre to return with enough pads to keep a maternity ward going for a week. The University doctor had insisted that I should go in and see her, and by the time I had answered all her questions, and promised to return if sitting the afternoon exam proved too much for me, there was just time for a quick cup of tea before returning to the exam room. There was no time to read my History notes; nor was there time to ring Frank as I had promised. He had had a hospital appointment that morning and, although I thought there was nothing seriously wrong, I did want to know, and I had promised to ring.

Later, I heard one of the other students describe the History paper as a 'swine'. He may have been right. I cannot remember much about it, except that at first I felt unable to answer any of the questions. Even before I opened the question book, the bit of confidence I had usually gained from my little trick of reading my brief notes was not there, and I didn't feel right. I told myself that I was being fanciful and that my notes, whether I read them or not, made no difference to the questions asked in the paper. The exam had begun, and I would just have to get on with it and do my best. I took a deep breath and chose a question that resembled one of the tutorial topics I had done some months earlier. Somehow, I managed to write enough to cover two or three sides of the paper with what I could remember of the tutorial paper I had prepared. Next, I made an attempt to answer a question on unilateral nuclear disarmament, which I felt I ought to be able to write on, because I had heard enough about it in lectures and discussions all year. In fact, all the questions were on issues which had been well covered during the previous months, but each one seemed more difficult to answer than the last. As the afternoon wore on, I felt more and more miserable. I looked up at the invigilator, who had been my final-year tutor. If I put my hand up, I was sure he would let me leave the room for a few minutes to compose myself. As I toyed with this idea, another thought crept into my mind. Suppose I did, and suppose that when I stood up to leave the room there was a repetition of what had happened at lunchtime. I decided to stay where I was. I had a go at the last two questions, feeling all the time that my writing was making no sense. At last, the exam, which had become an ordeal for me, was over. I waited until the room was virtually empty before I stood up. This time it was all right.

When I arrived in Great Harwood, Frank was waiting by the bus stop to give me his news: 'I've to 'ave another operation to get this lot sorted out. It's me gall bladder this time, but t'surgeon says I should soon be back to normal once it's been done.'

I felt sickened at the thought of him having to have a third operation so soon, but I joked, 'Well, it's to be 'oped so, or else they're goin' to 'ave to put a zip in your belly to save 'em t'trouble o' cuttin' it open.' I told him about my disastrous day and he tucked my arm in his comfortingly.

'We are a pair o' bonny buggers, aren't we, cock? Never mind, I'll make you a good pot o' tea when we get in, an' then you 'ave a good bath an' get to bed soon.'

I was thankful when that week came to its end. The two remaining English papers, Modern Drama and Shakespeare and Seventeenth-Century Literature, had proved less baffling than the History one, and I hoped to be awarded a pass, at least. The Politics exam was still to come, so if I did all right with that, and the dissertation, I might not come out of it too badly.

Whilst I had been swotting for my finals, Mary and John had sorted out their affairs and were now planning to move into a home of their own. Frank was to go into hospital at the end of June and, to his great disappointment, would not be well enough to come to the degree ceremony on 9 July.

'Think on. You'll 'ave to 'ave a proper photo taken for me,' he insisted. 'I want to see 'ow you look in that cap an' gown.'

I worked hard on my revision for the Politics exam and, when it was over, felt more optimistic about my chances. 'I gave it everything I'd got,' I told Frank, when he asked as usual. 'If I've failed that one, at least I'll know it's not for t'want o' tryin'.'

The results were coming out in the last week of June, a few days before Frank was going into hospital. I began to hope desperately, for his sake, that I had made it after all. I decided to stay at home on that day, for I knew the atmosphere at the

University would be tense, and I had enough tension to face in the days to come. I meant to wait until the following day before ringing in to see how I had got on, but suddenly I felt I could wait no longer. I picked up the phone.

'Congratulations, Mrs Bridges,' said a warm, masculine voice. 'You've got a two-two — you've done very well indeed.' I put the phone down and poked my head round the living-room door.

'Hey, you lot — I'm a BA! I've done it — I've got my degree!'

And so I had. It might only be a Lower Second, but it was a degree and I'd got it.

Soon, it was 9 July 1982, Degree Day, and I stood with my friends of the past three years, in the third row from the front of the congregation, at the degree ceremony in Maxwell Hall. Frank waited at home for the district nurse to come and take out the stitches from his latest operation wound. Margaret had phoned the night before from the maternity ward where she was in the early stages of labour. Sheila and Maureen had come with me, and were somewhere at the back of the large, crowded hall as I waited with the others for the speeches to end and the presentations to begin. It was surely the hottest day of the year. My thick, black gown felt heavy and uncomfortable in the stuffy atmosphere of the hall, and the too-large hood kept slipping sideways over one shoulder, so that the University colours of dark blue constrasting with pale blue and gold fell lopsided and untidy. My hair, so carefully done for the occasion, felt limp and sticky on my forehead, and I knew that my face, if I could see it, would be scarlet and shiny with sweat. Up on the stage, which was brightly decorated with banks of summer flowers, sat the members of the Senate, each resplendent in the regalia and colours of their own university. In the centre of the stage sat Professor Ashworth, the Vice-Chancellor, and, on either side of him, two distinguished local men who were to receive honorary Master's degrees.

One after the other, they read their carefully prepared speeches while I stood, hot and impatient, holding my cap in a sticky hand, trying to remember which side the tassel went, and hoping the darned thing would stay on my head long enough to see me out of the hall. I thought anxiously of Frank, and wondered if the nurse had been yet, and whether he had eaten the dinner I had left ready for him. We had had our own degree celebration at a quiet little restaurant the day after I had heard the results. As the waitress poured the wine, Frank had beamed at her: 'I'm not supposed to be doin' this, you know — eatin' all this red meat an' drinkin' wine.'

She gave him a puzzled look.

'No, but it's a special occasion, you see. It's t'wife 'ere, she's got a degree, an' I'm goin' in hospital at weekend, so we're celebratin' today.'

I could have crowned him with my plate of chicken and chips, but he looked so pleased and proud when the woman shook my hand and congratulated me that I thanked her politely and began to eat them instead.

All my relatives and friends in and around Great Harwood were so pleased for me. As I stood in Maxwell Hall, I fingered my special reward from Frank — an inexpensive yet precious ring, as a token of his love and pride. I had been inundated with cards and flowers; my O level friends had sent a message on local radio; my picture had appeared in the local papers; I had even received a letter of congratulations from the Principal of Accrington and Rossendale College on behalf of the staff. People stopped me in the street to shake my hand, and I was reduced almost to tears when one woman summed up the feelings of local people by grasping both my hands and telling me: 'You've shown it can be done — you've made us feel right grand!'

Professor Ashworth's voice broke into my thoughts. He was expressing the hope that we graduates would continue to play our part in the life of the Universtity as members of the Convocation. Sweat trickled down my forehead and steamed up my glasses; I whipped them off and surreptitiously wiped them on the inside of the left sleeve of the thick black gown. I thought of Margaret and hoped that her baby had arrived safely, and that the heat had not proved too much for her. Sheila and Maureen would be hot, too, having followed the University's advice about formal dress and worn smart suits for the ceremony. We had arrived to find that almost everyone else had dressed to suit the weather rather than the occasion. My girls, I thought smugly, looked smarter than anyone else, but I was so hot I would have stripped for twopence!

The Vice-Chancellor was talking about the cuts and their expected effects on the future of the University. He spoke of the campaign started by members of all the departments to alleviate these effects, and of the encouraging response to the campaign by industrial organisations and other outside bodies. I wondered, not very hopefully, if Barbara would agree to the children spending part of the coming summer holiday with Frank and Janet and little Leanne.

Suddenly everyone was clapping. I realised that the Professor had finished his speech and that already names were being called and the post-graduates in the front row were stepping up on to the stage to be presented for higher degrees. Soon it was the turn of my row. Someone at the foot of the stage straightened my wayward hood, and I climbed on to the stage as my name was called, to receive the congratulations of Professor Ashworth. Then I walked robot-like to the back of the hall to collect my degree certificate, and returned to my seat to join in the applause for my fellow graduates.

At the reception afterwards, I proudly introduced Sheila and Maureen to my friends and tutors. Going home on the express bus, we sat silent, tired after the long, hot day. In my bag was the receipt for my cheque from the official photographer. Hot, red-faced, and with steamed-up glasses, I had smiled at the camera for all I was worth. I might not look elegant, but I was determined to look happy, even if I died afterwards of heatstroke. It had all been worthwhile, I thought, as the bus sped through the familiar Lancashire towns towards Great Harwood and home. From that first night at the evening class, right through TOPS and the A level course and, finally, the University of Salford, it had not been easy, but it had been far more interesting than Highams' winding-room. There were some who suggested that it was a pity I had not had the opportunity to take a degree when I was young, but I had no regrets. After all, when I was at school all I had wanted was to be a working girl. Given the choice, I would not have had it otherwise. As things were, I had Frank and my grand family, I had met people I would never have come across in the ordinary way, and I had made many friends.

The goodbyes had been said, and the promises to keep in touch had been made. Some would be broken, but the memories would remain. We got off the bus at Church Street bus stop and walked wearily towards home. As we passed Highams, I thought of my old, dusty winding-frame, now, alas, no more. It had been dismantled some time before, and my fellow winders had been redeployed or made redundant. Dennis, I knew, still worked at the mill. I wondered fleetingly if he had been circumcised yet.

Frank was waiting for us, weary but smiling: 'We've got a new granddaughter, Win! Our Mag rang up, an' they're both fine. Sarah Jane, she's called. How've you gone on, cock?'

'OK, ' I told him, 'but I'm glad to be 'ome. A Degree Day baby!' I hugged him. 'I won't forget 'er birthday in a hurry.'

CHAPTER FOURTEEN

JUST A POSTSCRIPT

Sarah Jane, our Degree Day baby, is now five years old, and has begun *her* formal education at Berry Lane Infants' School, Longridge. As well as big sister Gemma, she has a little brother, John, aged four, and a one-year-old sister, Claire, and Frank and I are now grandparents to nineteen girls and nineteen boys.* 9 July 1982 was not the end of my academic career, for, in September of that year, I was given the chance to take a part-time post-graduate course at Salford for a Master's degree in History, under the supervision of John Garrard, who had supervised my BA dissertation. For this second degree, I recently completed a thesis entitled *Deference and Paternalism in the North-East Lancashire Cotton Towns During the Twentieth Century*. Once again, Frank is looking forward to a celebration and, this time, to our sharing Degree Day at Salford in July (1988).

And now comes the saddest and most difficult part of my story. In November 1982, young Frank died of a pulmonary embolism after a severe attack of pneumonia. The children had spent two happy holidays with him and Janet since Degree Day. They had planned to marry quietly when his divorce was made absolute, and it seemed he was to have a second chance of happiness. Somehow, this made his death seem all the more tragic. For a time, our family was like a body which had suddenly lost a vital limb. This sudden, unspeakable tragedy overshadowed all our failures and achievements and everything that had happened before. But, gradually, our lives began to mean something again. The pain of our loss may lie dormant for much of the time, but is always ready to come flooding back with a fleeting thought, a glance, or a familiar gesture which is a sudden reminder of him. But, as with my parents, there are the happy memories and, more tangible

* See Appendix A.

than memories, his children. Catherine, Mandy and Frank write to us regularly, and visit us annually during the summer holidays. To little Leanne, Frank and I are Grandma and Grandad and, on 9 July 1983, Suzanne Frances was born to Janet, a living legacy from our eldest son.

Life continues to be eventful. Soon after young Frank's death, we moved from our four-bedroomed council house to our present home, a small terraced house like the one I grew up in. Kevin and his girlfriend, Lynne, moved into their own home on the same day that we moved. This time, Frank joined me in giving his blessing freely, not caring for the opinions of others, wanting only to see them happy together. In September 1985, Maureen and Stephen were married. For the first time since our own marriage in 1950, Frank and I were alone. In February 1983, Frank went to the hospital for a check-up and it was discovered that he had what the surgeon described as 'a massive rupture' in his stomach. After yet another operation, he also suffered a pulmonary embolism and was taken to the hospital ward where young Frank had been. More fortunate than our son, with only one of his lungs affected by the clot, after several nightmarish days of anxiety for all the family, he began to recover.

'I thowt I were up wi', cock,' he told me as I sat by his hospital bed. 'I landed in this garden an' 'e were waitin' for me — I don't know whether it were St. Peter or 'oo the 'ell it were. But I towd 'im. I says, ''Nay, owd mon, you've 'ad enough off me an' I'm not ready yet, so you can bugger off!'' ' He grinned, looking at last like his old self, though much thinner and paler after his ordeal. 'An' that's when I started to get better,' he continued, 'an' you can start to get t'grub in, 'cause I won't be long before I'm 'ome.'

Our troubles were not yet over, for, since then, Frank has had yet another operation and has suffered a heart attack and a coronary thrombosis. At the end of 1984, he was officially retired from his 'job for life' on the grounds of ill-health. He now spends much of his time reading and driving me around to the centres where I teach adult students.

Oh, yes, I did find a niche in adult education, after all. In 1983,

I became involved in the Adult Literacy scheme run by Accrington and Rossendale College, and was offered part-time work as an assistant teacher. My first teaching experience was as an assistant in a Basic English class held in that very same laundry room where, just nine years earlier, I had myself returned to formal education. Now, I run two English classes at Great Harwood Adult Centre, where we cater for students ranging from beginners to those wanting to brush up their English in preparation for O levels. I also organise home tuition in the Great Harwood area for Adult Literacy students and for Asian women studying English as a Second Language. And I teach History in the Open College at Sandy Lane. Open College is a scheme specially designed for adults who want to return to education, either as a spare-time interest or on the way to university or polytechnic.

Through my work, I have continued to make many new friends among both students and staff. Frank has also made friends among the students who occasionally come to see me at home. Older friendships have remained strong. Dorothy, my persuader, is now a voluntary helper in my Monday evening English class, and a keen student in my Open College History class. Stella and I meet regularly as colleagues, for she also teaches Open College students. Although we do not meet as often as we would like, Jean, Veronica, Allison and I have continued to keep in touch since our TOPS days. I still receive letters and Christmas cards from some of the young students I met at Sandy Lane and at Salford, and I still enjoy a good 'camp'* with folk I have known since childhood when we meet in the street.

If anyone had told me on that Monday evening in September 1974, when Frank walked me up to the Adult Centre to enrol for English Literature O level, what it would all lead to, I would never have believed them. But then, if anyone had told me on that July day nearly forty-five years ago, when I left school to start at the leatherworks, that soon I would meet and marry Frank and we would have our large and loving family, I would not have believed them, either.

* 'Camp' is a local term for a friendly chat.

As I end my story, I can hear him moving about upstairs, for he has just woken up from his regular afternoon nap. Soon, he will come into the parlour where I am typing, to bring me a cup of tea.

'I've finished it, Frank,' I shall tell him. And, beaming all over his face, he will answer, 'Good lass, Win, I knew you'd do it.'

Appendix A

THE BRIDGES FAMILY

Our eleven children and, at the most recent count, 38 grandchildren are as follows:

Frank (1950-1982)	Catherine (1971), Mandy (1973), Frank (1977), Leanne (1980), Suzanne (1983)
Mary (1951)	Laura (1972), Heather (1976)
David (1952)	John (1969), Marc (1970), Bernadette (1971), Jeff (1972), Beverley (1973), Angela (1975), David (1977), Jim (1979), Joanne (1980)
Anne (1954)	Andrea (1972), Christine (1973), Daniel (1976), Katy (1982), Jack (1986)
Kathleen (1955)	Jamie (1976), Jon (1980)
Michael (1956)	Robert (1974), Christopher (1976), Michelle (1983), Michael (1985)
Eileen (1957)	Leanne (1975), Billy (1978), Stuart (1981), Rebekah (1984)
Margaret (1959)	Gemma (1978), Sarah (1982), John (1983), Claire (1987)
Sheila (1960)	Ben (1984), Joe (1986)
Kevin (1961)	Kevin (1983)
Maureen (1963)	

SEPTEMBER 1974

When I first enrolled for evening classes, I was working shifts as a winder in a cotton mill, one week from 6.00am to 2.00pm, the next from 2.00pm to 10.00pm. Frank was employed as a foreman in a potato crisp factory nearby. We had four sons and four grandsons, seven daughters and seven granddaughters. Five of our eleven children were still living at home in the four-bedroomed council house where Frank and I had brought up our large family: Eileen (17), who worked at the same factory as Frank; Margaret (15), Sheila (14), Kevin (nearly 13) and Maureen (11), who were all still at school. Michael (18) was living with his wife, Jean, and baby Robert in Waterfoot, Rossendale, about twelve miles from Great Harwood; and Anne (20) was living in Timperley, Cheshire, with her husband, Geoff, and two young children. The rest of our children lived near us in Great Harwood. Young Frank (24), his wife, Barbara, and their two children had their own home, while Mary (23), her two-year-old, Laura, and fiancé, John, shared John's parents' house. David (22) lived with Carole and their five children in a council house on the same estate as ours, as did Kathleen (19) and her husband, Andy. Just a few minutes' walk from our house was the cosy council bungalow where my Mum and Dad lived.

Appendix C

SOME POEMS FROM THE PAMPHLETS

A TRUE ROMANCE

When I was a girl I dreamed as girls do
Of the day I would meet my own man,
And when I grew up my daydream came true,
Which just shows that dreams sometimes can.
Soon we were wed and had our first boy,
A happy event we had planned,
We soon had a daughter to add to our joy
Then somehow things got out of hand;
For just a year later we had a new son
Not knowing what fate had in store,
And the year after that to add to the fun
I was waiting for child number four.
She was a girl, a real little peach,
Then her sister arrived premature,
Then with the next boy we had three of each
And enough is enough I was sure!
But I was wrong, and it was no surprise
When I came with the next gift from heaven,
Another young lady with father's blue eyes
Which brought up our number to seven.
Believe it or not the next year I'd none
But the year after that I'd a bumper,
Another wee girl, and before she was one
I'd another lump under my jumper!
She, too, was a girl, and when she was born
On a beautiful night in September,
I hoped that was it, but hope was forlorn
And our fourth son was born next November.
We soon had to move for the house was too small,
And the minute that we had moved in
"A new house a new baby!" my neighbours would call,
They just wouldn't let me get thin!
But the end was in sight for the next was the last,
It was Easter and she was a winner!
Now on each Easter Sunday we hold a march-past

And I take the salute before dinner!
Now don't get me wrong for I never would part
With one of my grand football team,
But to every young girl who has given her heart
My advice is "just watch what you dream"!

THE ANNUAL HORTICULTURAL SHOW

I cannot say I'm a grass widow, for grass is the last thing he'd grow!
I'm a horticultural widow, especially the week of the show.
I know I must try to be patient and try to be patient I will
Though I've got runner beans on the sideboard and onion sets on the sill,

The children keep pinching the pea-pods while I just pretend it's the birds,
He's carefully choosing tomatoes, I'm carefully choosing my words!
If I should be feeling romantic on a beautiful warm summer night
He says "If the weather should change dear, the potatoes will suffer
    from blight."

He took me down to his allotment, we strolled down the path straight
    and narrow,
We stopped for a while as with love in his eyes he gazed at his vegetable
    marrow,
If I venture into the garden the pansies are smiling with glee
And I know by their small cheeky faces, the cause of their laughter is me.

If I happen to slip while walking and land on the seat of my pants,
He'll say "Just wait and I'll pick you up AFTER I've watered my
    plants."
He's won second prize for the garden and here I am going to seed,
He's both Bill and Ben rolled into one and you've guessed it, I'm little
    weed.

But really, our garden is lovely with blossoms of every kind
And I'd just like to say, in spite of this rhyme, that of course I don't
    really mind.
I wish all the gardeners good luck at the show,
May they have the time of their lives
And when it's all over and they've had their fun
Let's all give three cheers for their wives!

NEVER WITH STRANGERS

If someone says "Come on with me,
I'll take you for a walk,"
I must remember Mother said
"To strangers do not talk,"

And even if I know them
I really must not go
Unless I ask my Mother,
For she's the one to know.

And if they say "It's quite alright,
Because I know your Dad,"
I must remember Mother said
That some grown-ups are bad!

I must not go away alone
Into the fields to play,
But stay near lots of people
And never go away.

Though really most grown-ups are good
And would not hurt a fly,
I must remember Mother said,
"If you are lost, I'll cry."

MOTHER'S DAY

I'm writing this on Mother's Day, it really has been grand
To have the gifts that came my way from each small, loving hand,
But though my heart was gladdened as I watched my children smile,
A part of me is saddened now it's quiet for a while.
For now my family are asleep, I've time to think of others,
And I seem to hear them softly weep, the poor Vietnam mothers.
For them there was no Mother's Day — only tears and sorrow,
No dreaming as their children play, for them there's no tomorrow.
For them no hope, no faith, no love; just bitterness and fear.
While bombs fall from the sky above destroying all that's dear.
Oh, when will men who crave for power learn to understand
A mother's joy to hold a flower given by a tiny hand?
The heartache when her menfolk go to fight a senseless war,
The helpless loneliness to know they may return no more.
Have they no hearts, these men who cause such grief, such sad despair,
Such hopelessness, when will they pause and think of those who care?
Of those who long to live in peace and treat all men as brothers,
To end all wars and thus release the poor Vietnam mothers.

JUBILEE LETTER

This is the text of my letter that was published in the *Lancashire Evening Telegraph* in June 1977:

Freedom of speech over the Jubilee

WHILE not condoning the childish antics of the Socialist Workers' Party in connection with the Silver Jubilee decorations, I feel bound to take issue with those of your correspondents who seem to imply that freedom of speech is a privilege to be exercised only by those who support the monarchy, and that anyone who disagrees with them is, at best, a miserable killjoy and, at worst, an unpatriotic moron.

If it is unpatriotic to feel that the colossal expense of the lavish spectacles shown on television this week, and paid for out of the public purse, is an insult to the intelligence of the public faced with increasing unemployment, falling living standards, unprecedented food prices and cutbacks in essential public services, then I am unpatriotic.

If the fact that victims of multiple sclerosis, heart and kidney diseases and cancer are often dependent on charity for the means to go on living seems to me more important than the sex of Princess Anne's unborn child or the identity of Prince Charles's future bride indicates that I am a moron, then I am happy to be a moron.

The street parties have given great pleasure to millions of children; the decorations have brightened many a drab scene; the Royal procession with its colour, pomp and pageantry was an unforgettable spectacle.

But the fact remains that, like the roast beef of old England, the monarchy has become a luxury that Britain can no longer afford.

M. W. BRIDGES (Mrs),
Springfield Road,
Gt. Harwood.

Degree Day, 1982.